Real Agent Advice

Real Agent Advice:

Your Source for Real Estate Agent Insight and Inspiration

Alex Saenger

Copyright Page

Real Agent Advice: Your Source for Real Estate Insight and Inspiration

Alex Saenger
20 West Gude Drive, Suite 200
Rockville, MD 20850
301-200-1232
www.AlexSaenger.com
www.RealAgentAdvice.com
inquiries@RealAgentAdvice.com

Published 2019.

ISBN-13: 978-0-578-43971-6

Dedications

There are so many people I want to dedicate this book to.

Of course, there's my family. Without the love and support of my wife and children I don't know where I would be. And of course, my parents, who inspired me to learn and follow my own path to life and success.

Also, of course, there are all the amazing people who took the time to be interviewed for the Real Agent Advice videos, some of which turned into this book. Every single one of you has my deepest gratitude. Thank you for taking the time to talk to the man with the camera...well, iPad anyway.

I would also like to dedicate this book to everyone in the Keller Williams family, especially Gary Keller. We truly are a family and I can't express enough the value of being here and the culture of sharing that made this book possible.

Lastly, I would like to dedicate this book to you the reader. Thank you for taking the time to read and learn from it. I am truly honored that you chose it. I know you will learn from the insights and that you will be inspired. Enjoy, and share it with your friends.

Quote

"Smart people learn from everything and everyone,
average people from their experiences,
stupid people already have all the answers."
~ Socrates ~

Table of Contents

Foreword

I met Alex Saenger back in 2014 when he left a boutique real estate brokerage and joined one of the launching offices in our rapidly growing network of Keller Williams franchises. He came to Keller Williams Capital Properties with a thirst for knowledge, a hunger to learn and grow, and a commitment to sharing what he learned with his fellow agents. As an experienced entrepreneur, who has built a company with a mission of transforming lives, careers, and communities through real estate, I have had the opportunity to see a number of highly successful real estate agents grow their businesses as we have built a company that closes over $2.4 billion in annual sales. I watched with pride over the years as Alex embraced the culture of KW and used what he was learning to consistently grow his business. In fact, he doubled his production in just two years and became a recognized leader in our local market and in the region.

Alex was also recognized across the region for his achievements, including a feature in Washingtonian magazine, and in April of 2016 he was recognized as the top sales person in our region of over 3,000 agents. His leadership was also recognized by his peers and he was selected to serve on the Associate Leadership Council (ALC) in our Rockville Maryland Market Center. For as long as I have known Alex, he has aggressively pursued learning and has been a leader with a passion to grow and share what he learns with others. Real Agent Advice is a perfect example of that. In Real Agent Advice, Alex outlines what he has learned from some of the top talent in the real estate industry and focuses on sharing great ideas and fundamental business practices that everyone should learn.

Alex interviewed some of the brightest minds in our industry like Jackie Ellis, Dianna Kokoszka, Wendy Papasan, my talented wife Kymber Menkiti, and rising stars like one of Realtor® Magazine's 30 Under 30 2016 award recipients Harrison Beacher, to name a few. Alex didn't just interview superstars though, he met with people at all levels of the business crafting a book that provides a diversity of perspectives on our industry all in one place.

This book is an excellent resource for people exploring a career in real estate, new agents, solo agents, or even members of teams that are in their growth phase. If you are committed to learning and growth, whatever your goals are in real estate, rest assured that Real Agent Advice is a valuable read and worth sharing with the people you care about in real estate.

Bo Menkiti
Operating Principal and Co-Founder
Keller Williams Capital Properties
Washington, D.C.

Preface

"What are three things you wish you knew, or someone had told you,
when you first got started in real estate?"

That simple question was the start of so much.

I eventually would ask that question, and similar ones, and dig deeper on the answers, to hundreds of real estate professionals from across the United States and beyond. Their answers became a video series (on YouTube or found at RealAgentAdvice.com), and many of those videos would serve as the basis for this book, Real Agent Advice.

Real Agent Advice is about you. It's about helping you, a current or prospective real estate professional. It's a snapshot in time of all the different stages of success captured in consumable moments and ideas. It's about letting you get advice from over a hundred real estate professionals, some who are just starting out and others who have achieved success, collected for you, all in one place. It's about giving you the answer to that simple question above.

I have been in the real estate industry since 2002. I am licensed in Maryland and Washington, D.C. I have a Master's degree in Information Management and a Bachelor of Science degree in Applied Mathematics/Statistics. I am certified as an SFR® and an e-PRO®. In 2015, I was the #1 agent in terms of total units sold and total volume for KWCP Rockville and the top agent for all of Keller Williams in Maryland in April 2016. I am also a Triple Gold Recipient for 2015, 2016, and 2017 from KW Realty International. I am a member of the National Association of Realtors®, the Maryland Association of Realtors®, and the Greater Capital Area Association of Realtors®. I have served on the Keller Williams Associate Leadership Council (ALC) for the past 4 years. I have served as an instructor for Ignite, an instructor for Real Estate Investing, and I am certified to teach Brian Buffini's Peak Producer course. I also used to teach marketing to MBA students at the University of Phoenix at their Rockville, Maryland campus and online.

In my career I have learned so much from so many. That learning took place over the years in so many different times and places. Real Agent Advice is about giving you, the reader, something similar, all in one place.

I firmly believe in educating both people within an industry and customers. Within my business philosophy, I talk about educating clients – even if they don't buy or sell a house from me. I believe that same philosophy applies to my fellow real estate professionals. That's why I put together Real Agent Advice.

Through Real Agent Advice you'll get to know me and over one hundred real estate professionals. And I would like to get to know you as well. If you want to talk about the book, something relating to real estate, or you'd like to send a real estate referral, you can get in touch with me. You can all me at 301-200-1232 or email me at coffee@RealAgentAdvice.com. I would love to hear from you!

ALEX SAENGER

Acknowledgements

I would also like to acknowledge some of the people who helped put Real Agent Advice together.

There is Zach Fletcher, the media manager for Saenger Group. Zach does too many things to name, and was the most instrumental person in the production of the Real Agent Advice videos and in the start of this book. He is the one who dissected all of the interviews and organized them into cohesive manageable parts. Without his work, there would be no book.

There is Derek Rebuck, who was a marketing assistant for Saenger Group. Derek, among his other talents, is skilled in graphic arts, and was the one who put together the images within the chapters of the book.

There is Mario Sakran, our book editor. Since I had never self-published a book before, Mario's ability to organize the process and take the video transcripts and turn them into something that actually looks like a book was amazing and critical.

I would also like to acknowledge all of my staff. You all do so much at Saenger Group which, directly or indirectly, helped me to put this book together.

I am sure I am leaving some people out. In a project like this it is hard to keep track of all of the people who may have made a contribution. Although I may not have listed your names, I would like to acknowledge anyone who played even the smallest role in this book.

Introduction

Welcome to Real Agent Advice: Your source for real estate agent insight and inspiration from over 100 real estate agents across the country. The interviews within Real Agent Advice reveal how to get motivated, be successful, generate leads, earn higher income and more.

In Real Agent Advice, you get real advice from real professionals. These are people in the real estate industry who have wisdom and insight to share. Their advice will help you as you travel along your journey in real estate.

Real Agent Advice is a collection of interviews with over 100 real estate professionals along with commentary provided by Alex Saenger, a 15 year veteran in the Maryland and Washington, D.C. metro real estate market. The book is based on videos located at www.RealAgentAdvice.com. The interviews have been edited for style and readability, but hold true to the conversations, ideas, thoughts, and messages.

For the interviews, Alex Saenger spoke with real estate professionals at all levels. He spoke with those at the top of their careers and those just starting out. Each interview started with one basic question, "What are three things you wish you knew, or someone had told you, when you first got started in real estate?"

The answers gathered present a diversity of viewpoints. Alex spoke with people who can inspire you and people you can relate to. He interviewed some people who are just like you, struggling with the same things you are. People who have been where you are now and have fought their way through the difficult times. And even some that are facing them now. People who have learned from both mistakes and successes. People who are eager to share their knowledge and experiences with you, so you can learn and share with others also.

Wherever you are in your career, you can find information in Real Agent Advice that can help you.

In this book you'll get advice about a number of topics including:

- The basics of being in the real estate profession.

- Having the right mindset for the real estate profession.

- Networking with other agents, business professionals, clients, and others.

- Why you need a database, what goes in one, and how it must be managed.

- The importance of lead generation and tactics you can use.

- The importance of using and mastering scripts to effectively communicate.

- Leaving your comfort zone and doing things that are difficult.

- The importance of how to put clients first.

- Joining a team if you're not on one, and managing a team if you're in charge of one.

- The importance of mentors and coaches and the difference between them.

- Things to think about when choosing which broker with whom to affiliate.

You'll get advice about all of these topics from professionals who took the time to share what they know. You'll also learn from the insightful commentary provided by Alex Saenger, reflecting on over a decade of real estate training and real life experience in the trenches of the business.

As you read Real Agent Advice, keep in mind that it's a book of advice. It isn't a manual. It won't teach you everything you need to know. Rather, it's a starting point. It's a way to get you to think about new things, to think differently, and to start seeking out more information. Real Agent Advice is about inspiring you with advice from real professionals so that you can start to move your career in a better and more successful direction.

Real Agent Advice will help you become aware of new ideas and new ways of thinking. You'll discover a new approach to narrow your focus on how you run your business and the potential to change your business going forward.

The professionals interviewed and highlighted in Real Agent Advice took the time to share their insights with you. Learn from what they have to teach.

We wish you the greatest success into the future as you move your businesses forward.

How to use Real Agent Advice

Real Agent Advice contains a wealth of information. How you choose the access it is up to you.

Of course, you could read Real Agent Advice straight through. In the book there is a progression of information, and this can be a great way to learn.

Alternatively, you could read the chapters in the order that you like. Let's say you need to learn more about databases, you could turn to that chapter first. If you want to learn more about lead generation, you could start with that chapter.

Another way to use the book, is to read each interview one by one. You could read one a day for instance. You could think about what the interview says, draw insights from it, and think about how to apply what you learned to your business.

If you really wanted to learn something in depth, you could study parts the book. You could move through a section slowly and take notes of what you learned. You could note things you want to learn more about and other books you might want to read. You could use the book as the first step in a broader education to improve your business.

Lastly, if you wanted to take an unconventional approach, you could use the topics and the conversations in Real Agent Advice as a starting point to ask questions of more seasoned agents. You could approach agents with what you learned and ask your own questions to get further insight. It could be a great way to open the door to further learning and to deepen your business relationships.

Whatever way you choose to read Real Agent Advice, be sure and read it again. As you grow in your business, the insights in the book will take on new meaning and you'll see them from a new perspective. Each time you read an interview, you can learn something new.

However you choose to read Real Agent Advice, it is sure to help you get on the path to improving your business.

REAL AGENT ADVICE

Chapter One:

Business Basics

Introduction

"Focus on fundamentals. Back to basics." These are things coaches tell athletes whether they are just starting out or they have been in a sport for a while. Basics are important.

In real estate, it is just as important to know the basics. Not just the basics of how to do the job, like how to understand a contract or how to list a property, but the basics of being in the business – the basics of what it means to be in the real estate business.

If you are just starting out or you are a seasoned professional, who is looking to get back to what is important in real estate, this chapter is for you.

This chapter is full of insight and inspiration from real estate professionals and is all about the basics of the real estate business. Through their words, and the commentary provided by real estate professional Alex Saenger, you'll get in touch with the fundamental ideas of being in real estate.

You'll learn about the extremely important idea of lead generation (it's so important there's a whole chapter in this book devoted to it), the idea of listings as a foundation for your business, and having a business focused on referrals.

You'll learn about three important C's: consistency, communication, and confidence and you'll get insight into spending your money wisely, time management, and the importance of models.

Professionals will also give insight into the importance of focus, planning, and knowing your numbers, and you'll get inspired to treat real estate as a business, know your worth, and focus on your goals.

You'll learn all these things, and so much more, from real estate professionals who took the time to share their thoughts. Through their experience you can get in touch with the basics of being in the real estate business.

So, whether you just got your license, or if you're looking to focus your career and get back to what's important, this chapter's for you. Sit back, read, and get into the basics.

Follow Up and Persistence

Gina Padro and Christine Whiteman, Garden City, New York

Gina Padro:

Follow up. I think follow up is the key to a very successful business. There is a lack of follow up in our industry as a whole. So if you are just 10% different, you're 100% better. Do your follow up.

Alex Saenger:

What does follow up mean to you?

Gina Padro:

Returning phone calls. Something as simple as returning phone calls. I can't tell you how many times I reach out to somebody, returning a call for an inquiry from a home and they'll say to me, "Thank you so much for getting back to me." For me, it's perplexing because you called me. I returned the phone call. Just our industry as a whole has a very bad reputation for not doing that. So, follow up with them. Return their phone calls. Make sure when you say you're going to call them back that you actually do, and provide the information that you say you're going to provide.

Christine Whiteman:

Pivoting off of that, I agree 100% with what Gina said. However, I think as a new agent, persistence and passion also come in to play with that, because if you're not persistent or passionate about what you're doing, a follow up will just fall apart.

Alex Saenger:

There's really not a whole lot to add. Follow up, make sure you return those phone calls, be persistent, and have a passion for real estate.

Why You Should Always Stay In Contact With Your Clients

Ada Wang, Houston, Texas

Ada Wang:

Focus and follow up are important. If you have a client referred to you, or you've been serving the client in the past, you always follow up, and focus on them for your time spent with them.

Alex Saenger:

So Ada talks about focusing on follow up. When you deal with a client, one of the most important things you can do is stay in communication with them. If you have a buyer and you're in the middle of buying a property, or if you have a seller, and you're in the middle of selling a property, one of the most important things you can do is, every week pick up the phone and give them a call.

Why? Even if there's nothing to report, it's much easier to give them that information and say, "Hey, guess what? No new news this week. Here are all the things that we're doing, but there's nothing new to report." Versus, doing nothing, waiting for weeks on end, and then they call you and that conversation is a lot longer. At that point, they're actually getting upset, because they haven't heard from you. So make sure that you focus on follow up, make sure that you call your clients, get in touch with them, and give them the information that they need. Make sure they're comfortable and confident that you're doing your job and you're doing it well.

30

Engaging With Your Community

Alisa Parrent, Anchorage, Alaska

ENGAGING WITH YOUR COMMUNITY

Alisa Parrent:

It's important to really absorb what everybody's doing around you. I got into the business a little bit self-taught and I think I felt like I didn't have the ability to talk to other people and find out what they were doing to be successful. I felt that would have been infringing on their territory. But I quickly learned that the more I engaged with people (agents and others in the real estate business), the more I learned. And that's an important aspect, to really learn from those around you.

Alex Saenger:

Anytime I run into an agent, an old colleague, maybe even from another broker, I always ask them, "Hey, what are you doing right now that's working? How are you getting your leads? How are you getting your properties sold? How are you getting your buyers? How are you getting your listings?" Really good agents will share that information with you. So take Alisa's advice and talk to other agents and find out what they're doing, that might help your business.

Coming From Contribution

Monice Ming Tong, Wexford, Pennsylvania

Monice Ming Tong:

I always tell my agents, "Don't go after money. Do the right thing, and business will come. If you go after the money, the money will run from you."

Alex Saenger:

What Monice is talking about is the law of attraction. It's interesting because if you come to a relationship from a place of desperation, the other person totally senses that feeling and is repelled by it. Whereas, if you come to the relationship from a place of contribution, from a place of focusing on actually caring about the other person, caring about what it is that they're interested in, and you're not focused on the money side of it or the transaction piece of it, it's amazing how close you could actually get with your clients and actually get referrals from them. This is because you are taking care of your client's needs, not your own. People are attracted to that.

So, make sure you don't chase the money, but instead chase the relationship. You're looking to build genuine relationships with all the people that are around you, most definitely with your clients.

Master A Few Simple Things

Pam O'Bryant, Washington, D.C.

Pam O'Bryant:

This is not a complicated business. It's not an easy business either. Master a few simple things at a really high level and you could earn more money in this business, with less money upfront, than anything else you could do. Best business in the world!

Alex Saenger:

In fact, out of Gary Keller's book, The Millionaire Real Estate Agent, at the very beginning, on page 22, it talks about the "big questions and the top of the world"[1]. It says, "Your approach, your ability, and your willingness to do the work of real estate sales will be the greatest determining factors for your success."[2] So if you want to be successful at this business called real estate, do a few things really well, and find a niche for yourself.

[1,2] The Millionaire Real Estate Agent by Gary Keller with Dave Jenks and Jay Papasan. Copyright © 2004 by McGraw-Hill Education

Real Business Basics: Back to the Essential Points

Katie Ruthstrom, Champaign, Illinois

REAL BUSINESS BASICS: BACK TO THE ESSENTIAL POINTS

Katie Ruthstrom:

So to me, it goes back to the basics. One basic is, you've got to follow your schedule. Two is, you've got to lead generate. Three is, you've got to surround yourself with talent. Talent is all about who you're in business with. Other major things that I've picked up on are go for listings, build habits, and focus on the activities. Those will bring the results.

Alex Saenger:

So Katie packed a lot of really great ideas into that interview. What I really want to focus on with what she talked about, from a business basics perspective - we go to The Millionaire Real Estate Agent book, by Gary Keller (pages 97 – 107) – are leads, listings, and leverage. "The three L's"[3]. She mentioned two of those in her interview. Without a solid foundation of leads, you're not going to have listings. Without having a solid level of listings, you're not going to be able to leverage. So make sure that you do all three of those things, the fundamental basic building blocks of a real estate practice, or you're not going to be as successful as you could be.

---

[3] The Millionaire Real Estate Agent by Gary Keller with Dave Jenks and Jay Papasan. Copyright © 2004 by McGraw-Hill Education

5 Things That You Should be Doing as a Real Estate Agent Every Single Day

Dianna Kokoszka, Austin, Texas

Dianna Kokoszka:

You have five things to do as a real estate agent. I call it the rule of five. Every day you lead generate. Every day you lead follow up. Every day you literally go on appointments. I don't care if you have one or not. Go make one. Go by and see a friend. Go by and see a for-sale-by-owner or an expired listing. The other part is every day you negotiate contracts. If you don't have a contract, role play it, because every day you role play. You do those five things every single day, and your success will be guaranteed. Now get to BOLD.

Alex Saenger:

What Dianna Kokoszka is talking about in this interview is that what you focus on expands. It's part of the BOLD (Business Objectives, a Life by Design) principles that she teaches in her course. I have to tell you, I took the course. I was blown away. It is one of the most powerful training programs that you could possibly take. It's the flagship of the KW MAPS Coaching (a coaching and education program for real estate professionals) experience. It really gets agents into production fast. In fact, in a recent year, people who graduated the program saw their number of transactions closed increase by fifty percent and the income of the graduates increased by one hundred and fourteen percent. It's something that people take over and over again, regardless of how long they've been in the business. Be sure to visit Dianna's Power Hour video blog on YouTube.

Why All Businesses Are Two Businesses

Jackie McKelvin, Littleton, Colorado

WHY ALL BUSINESSES ARE TWO BUSINESSES

Jackie McKelvin:

Something that I probably learned six months into my business, that was a game changer, is that I really signed up for two businesses. I signed up for real estate, and I signed up for lead generation. I had been doing lead generation pretty well, but I didn't have that mindset. Learning that I have two businesses helped me to shift it and to devote at least half my time to getting leads. I attended something with Ben Kinney and Tim Heyl, and that's where I really grabbed onto that.

Alex Saenger:

So, two businesses: real estate and lead generation. It really is kind of a profound thing to understand, when you get involved really in any business, that you really do have two jobs. One is the business that you're in, and the second one is in lead generation. Whether you're selling cupcakes, or cars, or anything else, lead generation, finding that customer, finding the person who's interested in your product or service is one of the biggest parts of any business. It's no different in real estate. In fact, the people that are the most successful in real estate are the ones that have systematically found ways to generate the biggest volume or the biggest number of leads. Because then they can pick and choose which leads they want to work on, and which leads they are going to pass on to the rest of their team.

So, if you're thinking about your business, think about the fact that on one side, you have the skills in real estate. The skills are what pay the bills. But, lead generation is the thing that actually generates the business so that you can apply those valuable skills.

Make Technology Your Friend

Willy Nelson (not the singer), Lee's Summit, Missouri

Willy Nelson:

Technology is your friend. I learned in the last year-and-a-half, that many of the people you're going to find that are looking to buy, you will find them through the use of technology. I really fought technology in the beginning but realized it was important. When I say technology, I mean it's anything "technology". For example, Facebook ads, and other types of social media, those kinds of things. In fact, to my surprise and delight, a third of my business comes from social media today.

Alex Saenger:

One of the most important things about technology is that you understand, that is where the world is headed (and already is). Yes, we're really going there, and we're going there fast. If you don't have a mobile app for your clients to use, you're missing out. If you're not on social media, Facebook, LinkedIn, Instagram, Twitter, you're missing out. That is where the millennials are. That is where the customers are.

Believe it or not, even that retired, 80-year old senior is on technology. The first thing that senior is going to do is look you up on the internet and see if you've got a website. Make sure you have a rocking website, you have a mobile app, and you're on Facebook, Twitter, Instagram, and some of these different social media sites, whichever one you're interested in. Make sure you're on there and you're present.

Business Comes From Referrals…Plain and Simple

Sally Masters, Naples, Florida

Sally Masters:

I do almost all my business by referral. I build great relationships with my clients and get lots of referrals from them. I get lots of referrals from other agents around the country too.

I just stay in touch really well with everybody. I do little "pop-by gifts". I stay in touch. Everybody I meet at a particular event might get a hand written note from me, and I make sure I stay in touch with them, to let them know that I'm in Naples. I cover Marco Island, Naples, Bonita Springs, Estero, and Fort Myers. So, if anybody has a client looking to buy or sell, I'm their person.

I'm also a luxury agent, one of the few down in that area. And I've been in the business so long, and I've lived in Naples for 36 years, so I know the area really well.

Alex Saenger:

So, just like Sally, my business comes to me predominantly by way of referrals. And those referrals can come from clients, and they can come from agents like you. And one of the things that I believe, just like Sally does, is the value of the pop-by gift idea. Because it's always better to give … before you ask.

With this in mind, I've put together the videos of Real Agent Advice, and this book, to give to you, so that you can gain some agent insight and inspiration. Hopefully, by me giving to you, you'll feel that it's okay for you to go ahead and reciprocate by giving me a referral for someone here in the Washington, D.C. metro area (D.C., MD & VA).

One of the things that I do whenever I go to a Keller Williams Family Reunion or Mega Camp, is I pop by with some gifts for the agents that I meet and interview. So, if you've been interviewed by me, you probably received one of the gifts that

I have.

One example of a gift is a little pouch. It says Alex Saenger of Keller Williams Capital Properties, Your Washington, D.C., Maryland and Virginia referral agent. With my phone number: 301-200-1232. It shows my office number, because I'm required by Maryland law to put that on there. And then it says, Real Agent Advice with Alex Saenger, and then, www.RealAgentAdvice.com. Inside, there is a little charging kit. It has a universal cord, a charging device, and one for the car as well. That's one gift that I've given out to people. That's pretty cool, and I think that most agents can use it every day.

Another gift is a little portable charger for your mobile phone, so that you can recharge your phone. And again, it says Alex Saenger of Keller Williams Capital Properties. It has my phone number, and it says Your Washington, D.C., Maryland and Virginia Realtor®.

These gifts are just a way to say, "… it was nice meeting you. Please stay in touch." It is also a constant reminder that I am there for them for any referrals in my area. If you received a gift like this, would you keep it or throw it away? That's right, you would keep it. This kind of marketing is certainly better than some big advertisement somewhere that people will forget about as soon as they pass it by.

Ask for the Business and it Will Come

Katie Harken, Denver, Colorado

Katie Harken:

Just asking for the business is so important. Ask for the business and it will come to you. Be comfortable asking.

Alex Saenger:

It seems pretty simple, right? Ask for the business. But most of the time, people don't actually do that. They just assume the people around them are going to know they're in the business. They're going to assume that just because they're related, that they're going to send them business. It's not the case. Asking for the business is one of the things that determines whether you're successful or you're not. The people that ask tend to do more business. It's just a fact.

Now, there are a lot of different ways you can ask. You can be very direct and ask for the business, or you can be more subtle about it. One of my favorite ways of asking for business is actually sort of that "Columbo" approach. Remember Columbo back in the day? He would always come in, he would talk to a person about whatever it was, and then right at the end, right as he was leaving, he would poke his head back in and say, "Oh sir, just one more thing." And that's when he actually asked the person what he was there for. This is a similar approach.

When you have a conversation about family, occupation, recreation, dreams (FORD), and so forth, at the very end of it, just ask, "Oh, by the way. Whom do you know that might be thinking about selling a house?" Be very specific, and ask that question if you're looking for listings, or, if you're looking for buyers, ask that instead. If you want to be general, you can just ask, "Whom do you know that might be thinking about moving in the next three to six months?" And most of the time, they'll say, "I don't know anybody, but I'll definitely keep you in mind." But occasionally, they will come up with the name of a friend, coworker, neighbor, or relative. They may even self-identify, and let you know they themselves have been thinking about moving. So asking for the business is really important. It's one of the things that turns regular agents into successful agents.

Creative Ways to Cultivate Consistency

Jeannie DeCarlo, Scottsdale, Arizona

Jeannie DeCarlo:

Consistency is important. Be consistent in what you're doing. Get focused and be purposeful. We are creatures of habit. Once we have really good habits then great things begin to happen.

Alex Saenger:

Sometimes it is hard to be consistent, but you have to find ways to manage it. If I get sidetracked because I have a new idea, I find it best to get the right kind of help. One thing about me is, I'm really creative. I come up with great ideas, but the fact that I can get you videos like I'm doing on a regular basis as part of Real Agent Advice (and turn them into this book), is not because I'm good at that. It's because I have people that are good at that. Whether you have to leverage someone else to be consistent, or you're really good at being consistent yourself, the most important thing to understand is that by being consistent and being in front of people at the right time, it will help you do more business. You never know when someone is actually ready to hear what you have to say. You need to constantly remind them you are there to help.

Just like you might not necessarily be listening to every one of my video episodes or reading every chapter in this book, the ones that you do listen to, or read, well, guess what? The fact that I'm consistent and I keep producing content you can actually relate to, eventually has you thinking, "You know what? That guy gave me great advice. The people he interviewed gave great advice. And you know what? I see his personality and I see that he's somebody that I can actually relate to, and my clients can relate to. He's somebody that I can give a referral to."

Remember, be consistent with everything that you do when it comes to real estate, especially with your lead generation activities.

How Creating a Win-Win Can Help Your Reputation

James Nellis II, Fairfax, Virginia

James Nellis II:

Understand that you need to create win-wins, because the person across the table from you, you'll see more than once if you have any longevity in the industry. Yes, there are a lot of times where there are multiple offers. In those situations, I'm pretty thankful we've been in business for over 30 years, because if they know our name, they're more likely to take our offer. This can happen even if it is the same or even less, than two, or three, or four, or five other offers. This is hugely important in our market.

Alex Saenger:

The first part of what James is talking about, is the win-win. So at Keller Williams, we have a philosophy of "win-win: or no deal", because when one side doesn't win they're going to be constantly fighting you to get that win back. With a win-win attitude, you start to build a reputation in the industry and the local market as someone the other agent is going to want to work with. Ultimately, if you've been in the business for a long time, like James talks about, what's going to happen is, people are going to look at you and they are going to think, "Hey, I've worked with that agent before. I can work well with that person. That agent creates a win-win for both our clients."

Not just that, but if you are in a multiple offer situation, like James talked about, and the seller's agent has worked with you before and has not worked with the other agents, you're going to have an edge. That seller's agent is going to want to work with you instead of an unknown entity, assuming that you created a win-win.

Make sure you take care of your reputation and build a positive one in your industry. That way when you run into any agents the second, third, or fourth time, they want to work with you, not someone else.

Your Commission – You're Worth It!

Alyson Hamel, Whitefish Bay, Wisconsin

Alyson Hamel:

For me, being stronger about my commission, being more in control, as far as that goes, and just putting my foot down and saying, "I'm worth it," is important.

Alex Saenger:

As real estate agents, it's illegal for us to talk about specifics about our commission, but one thing that we can talk about is knowing what you're worth. Understanding what you're worth and communicating that to your client is one of the most important things that you can do as an agent.

There's a saying that goes something like this: "In the absence of value, price becomes an issue." In other words, if you're not going to show those clients (whether they are buyers or sellers), the value that you're bringing to them, and why you're worth what you're charging, well, of course they're going to talk to you about what you're charging them (what your commission is) and what your fees are. They're going to be asking about that. They're going to be questioning it. Why wouldn't they? After all, in their minds, real estate agents are a commodity, everybody's the same. Right?

But you and I both know, everybody's not the same. Is the agent working as an individual the same as a team of six people? No, they're not. They bring a different value proposition to the marketplace. There's just as much value in both of them, but the fit for individual clients might be different, depending on what their need is. It might be how much hand-holding they want, how much processing they want, what kind of marketing they want, what approach they want to the market, or what that particular market or that particular house calls for. Understanding those things is really important. Understanding what your value is to your client, articulating that, and standing firm for what you believe, that's what the conversation around commission should be about.

Real Estate as a Business

Michele Mamo, Cincinnati, Ohio

REAL ESTATE
AS A BUSINESS

Michele Mamo:

Time blocking is really important. Also, you need to make sure that you're treating real estate as a business and not just as some kind of hobby. You need to be thinking, how real estate is a business. What does your money look like? Are you making the right decisions on hiring? Really sticking to that is important. Not wavering from it but being firm about it and not saying, "Well, it's okay to hire my cousin, or my best friend or somebody like that." That's what I would focus on for sure.

Alex Saenger:

So treating your business like a business is exactly what it sounds like. Don't treat it like a hobby. Don't treat it like a sport. Don't treat it like, "It's just something I can do." And certainly don't treat it like, "I'm just so good at this, I can just do it in my sleep." Treat real estate as a business because it is *your* business.

Time blocking is one way you can treat your business like a business. Time blocking helps you make sure you set aside time for every specific thing that needs to happen in your business. From lead generation, to client appointments, to actually working on your business plan, to meeting with your team. You have this all scheduled out through the whole week.

In addition she's talking about, "Oh well let me just hire my cousin because, well, my cousin's available." If your cousin is right for the job, sure, hire your cousin. But don't just hire your cousin just to hire your cousin. If you're going to think about being successful in business you want to go through the correct interview process. You want to do a KPA, or Keller Personality Assessment (or something similar), for every one of the people that you're thinking about hiring.

You might want to do a DISC Profile to see how they fit within the dynamic of the team. Are they an outgoing, driven kind of a person, or are they a more conservative, very numbers oriented person? Depending on the role that you have, you might want to pick a certain person for a certain role and with a certain type of personality. And the Keller Personality Assessment's going to help you also identify where they would best fit within your team. Don't just hire your cousin because you like them. In fact, a lot of times, what I've found is, the people that I'm the most like are probably not the people I need. I need people doing things that are not the things that I like doing. They're going to have a different personality and a different skill set than I have.

Why You Should Play Red Light, Green Light With Your Finances

Cheryl Coleman, Huntington Beach, California

Cheryl Coleman:

To know how much money you need to make, you need to treat real estate like a business. I have a board in our office so everybody knows, in order for you to get paid (like my assistant), we need to at least make this much money. This is our break-even point. That was an exercise I did last year. I had to really put my expenses where I could see them. I was afraid to look at them, but after I did I was like, "No wonder there's so much money in your bank. You're really good at red light, green light."

So, now the whole team knows. This is what we need to make to break even. If we don't make that, then we might not be able to keep our assistant, so …let's get to work!

Alex Saenger:

So, red light, green light is exactly what it sounds like. Don't have any money? You have to stop, you can't spend it. Red light. Got money? Green light, you can spend it. It's not just red light, green light with whether you have money or not. It's a question of do we want to move forward with this thing? Is it something that's actually going to generate revenue for us or move our mission forward? Is it something that's going to increase our bottom line?

Now, in Cheryl's case, she's looking at it in terms of how much money do we need to make as a baseline just to support our staff? Obviously, that's really important. In addition, you're going to want to have a reserve. So on those months where you don't quite make enough money to do what you want to do, you've got some money you can spend. At the end of the year, you need to have a plan that's going to make sure that you can cover the entire year for all of your staff, all of your employees, all of your expenses, and make sure there's a profit.

What to Spend Money on When You First Get in the Business

Cole Whisenhunt, Lubbock, Texas

Cole Whisenhunt:

Early on, you get a ton of advice, or you're in the office and you hear this agent's just knocking it out of the park with open houses. That one's doing door knocking. This one's doing mail outs. And so, for a while I just thought, "Man, I've got to try it all." So, I just started spending money everywhere instead of focusing in on one position. If I could go back, I would say, "I'm taking all my money. I'm putting it into my database. I'm going to feed that systematically and let that grow as big as it can be." I would either hit a ceiling or cap out, and get to a point where we had to add somebody else on the team before I moved on to spending money in all different directions and trying it all.

Alex Saenger:

When you get into real estate, how you spend your money is really important. One of the first places you should spend your money is actually in your database. Some real estate websites, even some promoters who use social media, want you to spend your dollars on their product to get leads. The fact of the matter is, the best source of leads is going to come from your database and having a systematic approach to communicating with them. After all, would you rather spend $2000 with a social media platform or a real estate website where they might send you a bunch of inquiries, or would you rather spend that money with the people that know and love you and trust you in real estate? People who are able to actually connect with you on a personal level and might want to actually send you referrals?

So, maybe you do a client appreciation event or maybe you have coffee or lunch with somebody. Spend that money on the things that matter most. Spend the money on your database, get the revenue, and build a base of actual finances so that you can fund everything else. Once you've built your database set up on a systematic approach, then you can explore other options.

Why You Need to Identify Your Natural Abilities

Nancy Bennett, Walnut Creek, California

Nancy Bennett:

Natural ability? I think, if you start with natural ability and, for some people, it's coming from a place of serving. For some people, they are social butterflies. For some people, they're in it for the money. I think it's a combination of talents, what you have naturally and what you can build on. Get educated.

For myself, I'm a social person. If we're talking about the Keller Williams DISC system, I have a high "I" with a just as high "D" – I'm very sociable but also very driven. We're going to have fun but we're still going to make our numbers. Somebody else in my office may be very process-oriented, talk a little bit slower than I do, and really connect on a different level than maybe the I's and the D's of the world. I've seen them be extremely successful as well. It's a combination.

Alex Saenger:

Before you can really tap into your natural ability, you first have to be self-aware. Know what you're good at and know what you don't like doing. Focus on those things that make you good at what you do and embrace that. Make that most of who you are and incorporate that into your business. Your business will be most successful when you're leveraging yourself and your abilities to the greatest extent.

Push off those things that maybe you don't like doing or maybe you're not good at. Push those off to somebody else. Let somebody else work for you and leverage that person and leverage yourself in a way that allows your business to be successful through self-awareness and natural ability.

Write Down Your Goals and Take Steps Towards Them

Angie Fucigna

Angie Fucigna:

For me, it has been baby steps. It could be something very small. For me, fitness it very important. I started running two years ago. I didn't know that I could do it. Then I started running 5K's. The first year I did it, I said I want to run six 5K's in a year, and I did. Just proving to yourself that something can be done is important. It doesn't have to be something big. It's just putting your mind to it. It's changing your mindset, and just going for it, and persevering. Perseverance and persistence are important.

Alex Saenger:

Lou Holtz said, "If you're bored with life, if you don't get up every morning with a burning desire to do things, you don't have enough goals." He's not the only one that talks about goals. People like Brian Buffini, Dave Ramsey, and Tony Robbins, all of these people talk about goals. It's really interesting because we can have a conversation about goals, but never do anything about it. The bottom line is, if you actually write your goals down and communicate them to others, you're more likely to achieve those goals than if you don't. In fact, one of the things that we do a lot in life is we have an idea of what we want. You know what you want. Maybe you want a new car. Maybe you want a new house. Maybe you want a vacation. Just taking a picture, an image of that, and sticking it up somewhere where you see it every day is one way to really connect with your goal.

In my case, my goals are very defined. They're part of my business plan. Those goals are written on a sticky note and stuck right on my monitor. That way, I know every day walking in I'm looking at that goal. I know exactly what it is and what I need to do to get to it. If you haven't written down your goals, make that a priority for yourself today. Write down those goals and you'll be surprised at the end of the year, if you reference those goals consistently, how much more likely you are to achieve your goals.

A Fresh Take on the Importance of Listings

Patrick Hammonds, San Antonio, Texas

A FRESH TAKE ON THE IMPORTANCE OF LISTINGS

Patrick Hammonds:

The best advice that was given to me was to focus on listings. I felt like I really wanted that sense of urgency, the microwave generation. I focused on buyers because I thought they're ready to do something right now, whereas sellers are just sitting on the market, spending money up front. If I had a different school of thought on that in the beginning, it's interesting to imagine where I would be today in my career, because that would have changed everything.

Listings, they're important because they free you up for time. We talk about leverage all the time through people and through all these different sources, when in reality, leverage can simply be you not focusing all of your time on one person, or spending six hours driving around. When you have those listings, the clients are coming in, so you've leveraged a lead source essentially for free. You've leveraged future listings for people that are considering selling because they see your sign in the yard, and you've leveraged that house itself online, so now you've got web leads too.

Basically, listings run your entire business. When they said, "List to last," boy, they had that right and that's another case of not reinventing the wheel.

Alex Saenger:

Probably one of the oldest sayings that Patrick brought up in his segment here was, "You have to list to last." In Gary Keller's The Millionaire Real Estate Agent book he addresses this very specifically. In fact, in the book on page 16 he lists listings as, "The High-Leverage, Maximum-Earning Opportunity."[4]

---

[4] The Millionaire Real Estate Agent by Gary Keller with Dave Jenks and Jay Papasan. Copyright © 2004 by McGraw-Hill Education

Why would you say that is? Because, as it says on page 102 of The Millionaire Real Estate Agent, "Seller listings mean marketing opportunities"[5] for you as an agent. Some of the opportunities it describes include: a sign of yours is out in front of the property, you're in the MLS (Multiple Listing Service), and you're on the internet. You're all over the place getting exposure from that listing. You might send out postcards or knock on doors around it. You have more control over your time. When you're dealing with buyers, you're spending a lot of time and you're on their schedule. When you're dealing with listings, you set the schedule, you set the pace.

The book also mentions on page 102 that, "Seller listings maximize your per-hour compensation"[6], because you can carry way more listings than you can buyers. "Volume, volume, volume."[7] Again, if you look at how much volume you can do from a listing perspective as an individual, or even as part of a team, you can do way more business on a listing basis than you can on a buyer basis. It's just a matter of doing the math on your time.

When you do a listing, you have to do all the CMA comparisons, the comparative market analysis, for that property, so you know everything that's going on around you. You're also the one that gets to set the price that starts the conversation with the market. So you're in front of the price element with listings.

Finally, if you market your property well, you're probably going to pick up a buyer from that listing. Which is one of the reasons, why if you focus on listings, you can actually start to build a team pretty rapidly. This is because, every listing you get should turn into another buyer that you're going to get. Having a buyers' agent on your team is how this is an element of leverage. It's how you can build more business and not sacrifice what you're doing to earn a living.

[5, 6, 7] The Millionaire Real Estate Agent by Gary Keller with Dave Jenks and Jay Papasan. Copyright © 2004 by McGraw-Hill Education

Use Listings as Leverage and Watch Profits Rise

Marshall Johnson, Reno, Nevada

Marshall Johnson:

Listings are everything. Listings are leverage.

Alex Saenger:

There's a saying in real estate, "You've got to list to last." Listings, as he mentioned, are leverage. Why? Because the wonderful thing about listings, are you take the listing, you do the right amount of marketing, right up front, and you put it out there and while you're doing something else, other agents are showing your house. They're showing your listing. They are using their time to go ahead and get people into your listing. More than likely, they're the ones that are going to be bringing you an offer. Now, of course, you can also use listings as leverage to get more buyers through open houses and contacts made online or by phone about that listing. If that listing isn't a good fit for that buyer, you can always show them something else and secure a new client.

Listings are one of the keys that actually makes your business thrive. In addition, with a listing, most of the time, we can stick a sign out in front of it. You can also have directional signs pointing to that listing. Listings really become one of the most critical components if you want to be in the business for a long time. Just imagine a street where there's 100 houses and 10 of them have your sign in front of them. What kind of a powerful statement is that going to send? Making sure that you have listings and making sure that you leverage them is critical to your success.

Basic Lead Generating in Open Houses

Angie Smart, Gainesville, Georgia

BASIC LEAD
GENERATING IN
OPEN HOUSES

Angie Smart:

Make sure to do open houses. I was never a fan, but I have become one lately. I think it's a huge place to get not only buyer leads, but sell your houses quickly.

So here you are. You're in a neighborhood. The people who are going to come to the open house, more than anyone else, are the nosy neighbors, right? So this is a great place to pick up more listings in that neighborhood (from nosy neighbors who may also be thinking of selling). Also, buyers that come, might be planning to sell their house as well. So it's a good place to pick up listings, not just buyers.

Alex Saenger:

So open houses. There are a lot of different ways to use an open house. Number one, the more open houses you do, the more likely you are to pick up a potential buyer that doesn't have an agent. The lower the price point, the more likely they are to not have an agent that they're working with. The higher the price point, the savvier they tend to be, and they may have gone through a transaction before and have a relationship with an agent. So, if you're a new agent looking to work open houses from another agent that's more experienced, that maybe has coverage issues, go ahead and grab those open house opportunities. Try to focus on the lower tier price points, maybe mid-to-lower tier, and especially the very first open house for a specific listing, or an open house where there's a price reduction. Those tend to be the most heavily visited open houses. So that's number one: open houses are great for picking up buyers.

Number two, Angie mentions open houses are great for picking up listings. I just had an open house, and at that open house, we had 34 groups come through. It was a great open house, the property was priced exactly where it should be, because the condition and everything else was just right. I had five different neighbors that stopped by, with two that said they were planning on selling within the next three years. So, I put them in my database and added them to a drip campaign. I make sure that I'm inviting them to events I have, but more importantly, now I have a lead. Yes, it's not a lead for right now, but it is a lead that builds my pipeline for two or three years out. Also, it's one of the best ways to build a farm of potential clients in an area.

The more you do open houses in the same area or the same neighborhood, the more you start to see the same people coming through those open houses. And you start to build a relationship with those people. "Oh, you haven't found a house yet? Well, great, maybe you should give me a call, because I'm the one that seems to be listing all of these houses, and you might find out about them before they go on the market. Wouldn't that be great?" "Wow, never thought about it that way, Alex." "Yes, well, maybe you should be talking to one of my buyers' agents."

So there are lots of different ways to use open houses. The last one that I'll throw at you is one that I use a lot. It is, whenever I put a house on the market, I do a lot of upfront marketing. I draw a ton of people to the open houses. I don't do it from 12 p.m. to 4 p.m. though. I do my open house from 1 p.m. to 3 p.m. I keep it to a very short window, because I want to make my open houses a priority. By doing that, I kind of create a "frenzy" effect. The idea is to bring in lots of people and have them kind of fighting each other for that house, so you can get, not one offer that beats you down, but get multiple offers and go up from there.

So there are a lot of ways to use an open house. The ones discussed here are just a couple of examples.

Free Resources at Your Fingertips

Teresa Souvignier, Palo Alto, California

Teresa Souvignier:

I think I would go on to KWConnect (the internal KW resource for information, content, and training) and watch more of the videos, because there's a ton of resources on there to help you with all kinds of things that I was insecure about. Even if you can't find someone to shadow all the time, you can get online, go on KWConnect, and learn from there.

Alex Saenger:

One of the things that's awesome about Keller Williams is that they have a backend system called KWConnect. It's where agents like myself, can post information and content so that other agents can benefit from that advice. Now, it's not just limited to video, there's plenty of content including all of the training that we provide at Keller Williams. By the way, we are the number one training organization in the world after all. So all the resources and training that we have are available through KWConnect.

But, in addition to that as a resource, you as an individual agent can reach out on YouTube. There's plenty of content from lots of different people, lots of different coaches, and lots of different agents that are providing advice, that you can take advantage of.

Or, if you haven't done so already, make sure you go back in the library from the Real Agent Advice videos and take a look at some of our episodes. There's lots of great content. And not all of it is found in this book, since we keep adding fresh content weekly.

If you're not sure about where you should be or what you should be doing, or maybe you're not confident about something to say or do, reach out to the information you have available through Real Agent Advice, through KWConnect, or YouTube. Tap into the content in this book. Use these resources and make sure that you get the information you need to be confident in the marketplace.

Time Block With Wiggle Room

Mercedes French, Huntington Beach, California

Mercedes French:

Time blocking is incredibly important. If you don't time block, your whole day disappears. At the end of the day, you know you've been busy moving, moving, moving, but you haven't really produced what you should have because you didn't have an organized system in place. So I would say time blocking, along with systems and processes, are very important.

Alex Saenger:

So, I think at this point we all know what time blocking is, right? You have your lead generation time in the morning, and then you have time set out to do your marketing. You have time set out to meet with clients, make appointments, and things like that.

One of the things that isn't discussed a lot with time blocking is the idea of wiggle room, because as agents we know that our days never go as planned. We always get that curve ball thrown in, either by a team member or by a client or something like that. So it's important that when you build your schedule for the week, and you have a consistent schedule with your time blocking calendar, that you build in chunks that are specifically designed as wiggle room.

Now that might be, you need to run out to the dentist. Or maybe you need to put out this fire for a client, or maybe brochures need to be printed and extra ones taken to the property. Whatever it is, make sure that you add in wiggle room in your time blocking.

Why You Should Have a Specific Area of Focus

Randy Antonio, Kahului, Maui, Hawaii

WHY YOU SHOULD HAVE A SPECIFIC AREA OF FOCUS

Randy Antonio:

I always tell new agents, if I were to start over I would probably go very narrow and deep in a territory and be a specialist in that particular area, or maybe it's a condo building. That would really keep you razor-sharp and focused and that's a good thing to be.

Alex Saenger:

Have you heard the concept of there are riches in niches? Well, that's kind of what Randy is talking about with focusing on a specific area. Now, a specific area could be a geographic farm area, where you're focused specifically on a neighborhood, or, like he said, a high rise building, and you're becoming an expert on everything related to that building or to that area or community. That might mean knowing the parks that are nearby, the groups that get together, the restaurants, whatever it is that makes that particular lifestyle for that community or that building unique. That's what you become an expert on and that's why people come to you.

Now, another area that you might focus on might actually have nothing to do with geography. It might have more to do with what your own interests are. So, for example, I like to invest in real estate. So I started a Meetup group focused on real estate. And guess what? At the last meeting we had, I picked up a brand new investor who's looking to invest in not just one property a year, but five to ten properties a year for the next five years. That's doing something that I enjoy. Another colleague of mine, here in the office, guess what? She's a vegan. I said, "What a great opportunity to start a group. Get together once a month or once a quarter with a bunch of vegan friends. Start up a Meetup group and share recipes. Do something like that and then you can bring real estate into it as well."

So, if you're thinking about where to start or you're struggling with where you are, think about narrowing your focus and finding a more specific area where you can build relationships, and through those relationships, get more business.

Know Your Market

Lee Potts and Barbara Potts, Kahului, Maui, Hawaii

Lee Potts:

In Maui, we have a lot of second home buyers, and a lot of our products are what we call "condotels". They're like vacation rentals. You need to know how associations work, you need to know how vacation rentals work, and you need to know how to finance those things. You need to know what's for sale and where the issues are. That's what you need to know.

Barbara Potts:

And we have all kinds of other fun little quirks with non-permitted issues and just a lot of other different issues for people that live there and homes that get sold.

Alex Saenger:

I think it's really important to know your specific market. Know what's in, what people are after, and how you can help them. Finances are not the same in every type of market. Second home markets, well, they require either a second mortgage or a second home loan or cash. And that's a different market than a primary market, with maybe a VA loan or an FHA loan. Understand the specifics of what your clients are looking for, even within an area where you might have pockets that are different. Knowing those differences, talking to financial people, driving through the neighborhoods, talking to neighbors, and really getting to know your specific area is one of the best ways you can serve your clients to the best of your ability. And that's really why your clients are coming to you.

They're coming to you because you're an expert in that local market. Make sure you tour every home you can so that you understand not only the general sense of what's happening in the market, but the specifics of a particular neighborhood, some of the amenities, some of the different characteristics of the community's homes, and what the standard layout looks like. Things like that really help you understand the nuances of a particular area and allow you to best serve your clients.

Planning Your Business Ahead of Time

Heidi Fore, Louisville, Kentucky

Heidi Fore:

Planning your sales and your income 90 days out is important. If it's currently January and you're thinking about real estate sales, think about what's going to be closing in March, because the things that you do in January will impact the number of closings and therefore the income that you have in March and April. Things happen 60 to 90 days out in real estate. The activities that you do now don't show up as results until 60 to 90 days from when you did them.

Alex Saenger:

So when Heidi's talking about planning your business about 60 to 90 days out, that means your budget, your results, your closings, and everything that you're doing. You want to make sure that you have enough cash reserves for 60 to 90 days into your business, especially if you're just getting started.

You also really need to focus on the activities, not the results, because the work that you do today may not show up for 60 to 90 days in terms of leads that might come in or business that you might get.

Know Your Numbers

Alyson Hamel, Whitefish Bay, Wisconsin

Alyson Hamel:

I need to know my numbers and statistics more. I think yesterday, when we were taking the bus to Houston, we did a little Mastermind, and everyone knew their numbers, just like that. I think having that mindset going back home, that's going to really help me grow my business.

Alex Saenger:

What does "knowing your numbers" mean? Well, in the KW model, in the KW world, we go back to our favorite book, The Millionaire Real Estate Agent by Gary Keller. If you turn to page 131 -- if you have a copy, turn to page 131, go ahead, do it right now -- if you look at the model, it's going to tell you. In using the model, I usually start at the bottom and work my way backwards and work my way back up. So, if I want to make $200,000, and I want $100,000 to be from sellers and $100,000 to be from buyers, and I know what my average commission is for each, and I know what my selling price average is for each, then I can start working backwards up the model and figure out how many units I need to actually sell in order to get $100,000 in gross commission income for sellers, and the same thing for buyers.

And not only that, but I'm going to have to figure out what's my rate of conversion. So, in business, if I get a seller, how many times do I get a seller who falls out? Maybe 25% of the time. So, I actually need four sellers in order for three to close. This shows that you're going to have to figure out what your rate of conversion is.

Before that, we had to get the property under contract. And before that, we actually had to get the listing agreement signed. And before that, we actually had to have appointments. So it all filters back up to how many appointments you need to have.

For example, let's say you wanted to do 48 transactions a year. Let's also say, that through all the different conversion rates, you've realized it's really like a two to one ratio. If you wanted to do 48 transactions a year, 24 for sellers and 24 for buyers, and you need a two to one ratio, that means you're going to need to have one buyer and one seller appointment every single week in order to achieve 24 transactions at the end of the year for each one of those, for a total of 48 transactions (buyers and sellers combined). That's assuming you're actually going to have a life and go on vacation, and not just work 52 weeks of the year.

That's what the model shows you. That's what knowing your numbers is all about. Having that information at the tip of your tongue is really going to help you figure out exactly what you need to do to generate the business you need and to reach the financial goals that you have for the year. Without knowing those numbers, you're kind of swimming in a circle. Let's get you on a straight path to success. Let's get to know your numbers.

Why You Need To Know Your Documents Inside Out

Pam O'Bryant, Washington, D.C.

WHY YOU
NEED TO KNOW YOUR
DOCUMENTS INSIDE OUT

Pam O'Bryant:

Somebody told me earlier that mastering the paperwork would make everything easier. Really understanding the contract, the clauses, the buyer agreements and the listing agreements, and really what they said, and that, by learning a few basic scripts and dialogues, my life would be a lot easier.

Alex Saenger:

Understanding your paperwork is such a critical component to being a professional real estate agent. As Joe Niego says, "It's the skills that pay the bills." Understanding your paperwork is one of those skills.

When you have a client who is going into a particular paragraph and wants an explanation, you have to be prepared to explain exactly what that means. Not just what that means but how you can manipulate that content to the client's favor, depending on the particular situation you're in.

For example, do you want to have a delayed settlement or do you want to have an earlier, fast settlement? Understanding the paragraph that goes with that piece of information is critical to getting your clients exactly what they want.

Working by Referral With Models

John Pace, Richmond, Virginia

John Pace:

One thing that really worked for me in the past, was that I was a Brian Buffini guy for eight or nine years. I followed his model on how to build your life by referral, and your business by referral, and that was a game changer as far as getting my business set up. I wish I had followed The Millionaire Real Estate Agent book as far as building my business up. That would have been the one thing that probably would've accelerated my business two or three times faster … if I had followed that model.

The wow didn't happen until about four years after reading the book, and that is, we all had different businesses, but the model works across different types of business. Whether you're referral, whether you're internet lead based, or something else, just follow the model. I came into it thinking, "Sure, but my business is by referral, so that's not going to work for me," and so I tried to get creative with the model, and that's when I messed things up. It's a proven model for a reason.

Alex Saenger:

I can relate to John, because when I first started, I focused on getting trained. My broker, well … they didn't have any training. So I had to go outside the broker and find training. That's where I discovered Brian Buffini and the Peak Producers system that he has. I took the training and I doubled my business. It was fantastic!

But then I hit a plateau. I hit another level where I couldn't seem to break through, a place where I had a natural level of achievement. When I finally discovered The Millionaire Real Estate Agent book, and all of the systems and models that they had in there, I realized that my issue wasn't my natural ability or working by referral. My issue was I didn't have a foundational system or a foundational model for my business. Once I implemented that system and model, based on The Millionaire Real Estate Agent book, boom, I doubled my business again.

But then again you wind up hitting another plateau. Why? Because now you have to refine those systems and refine those models so that you can break through to another level. You have to introduce leverage in the way of people. You have to introduce leverage in the way you do things with systems. Understand that learning how to sell real estate and how to get leads is important, but it's equally, or even probably more important, to implement those systems and models to help your business grow even further.

The Tools of Our Trade

Mike Brodie, Plano, Texas

Mike Brodie:

My advice is, this company (KW) is built on systems and models. They work and we know they work. You should use them and follow the training and the tools and the coaching that we have. It's almost a can't-miss. The reason KW is number one in the world, in so many categories, is that we have a system, and we have scale. We have brand. We have the best toolbox in the industry. And we've got great leadership at all levels. So good luck to you, God bless, and all the best.

Alex Saenger:

So the question I have for you today is this: If somebody could show you exactly how to be successful in real estate. Exactly. The exact path that you need to take to be a huge success in real estate -- would you listen? Would you take that into consideration in terms of making your plan to be successful? Well, I did. And the reason my business is off to its best year ever, is because I've decided to implement the systems and models that Gary Keller put together in The Millionaire Real Estate Agent book. It's not just a book, it's a culture, and it's a language. It has systems and models that you can follow to make your business the best it can possibly be.

Now, Mike talked about scale. The wonderful thing about the models in the book, is they're scalable. No matter what level of business you're doing, you're going to be able to apply the same principles. Whether you're an individual agent, a team of 10 people, or you're doing an expansion team, or you're opening up your own office, you are able to apply the same principles. All the systems and models that are defined apply no matter what your level of business.

In addition, Mike mentioned the toolbox. One of the things that as real estate agents we struggle with, is making sure that we have the right tools at the right moment. You might think, "We're not building a house. I don't need a hammer and a screwdriver." But a script is a tool just like a hammer. A presentation or a piece of marketing is a tool just like a screwdriver. A virtual reality 3D walkthrough of your listing is a tool just like a laser guided double bevel sliding compound miter saw with 15 amps, and a 12 inch blade (all right, maybe not – but if you buy a compound miter saw, get one with a laser guide). And being able to pull out those tools at the right moment when you're in a conversation with your clients or prospects is important. Maybe though, you're not pulling out one of those tools. Maybe you're pulling out a tool like The Millionaire Real Estate Investor book. That's a tool that we have, that we can share with our clients who are thinking about investing.

When you think about where you are now and where you want to go, there are proven systems and models to get you there. There's a proven path that's been blazed ahead of you. All you have to do is follow it and you'll have great success.

Are You a Designated Agent?

Dalia "Dee Dee" Cortez, Corpus Christi, Texas

Dalia "Dee Dee" Cortez:

When I started in real estate, back in the day, the first thing my broker told me, was that if I was going to go to school, that I should earn my designation. Apply and pay for designation. At this moment I have my TAHS, which is your Texas Housing, for Texas, my GRI, my ABR®, my CRS, and my SRS. You name it, I have it. Because every time I had to go to school, to renew my license, I would prefer to spend my money on having a designation that could back me up in the future.

Alex Saenger:

So what is a real estate designation? It's basically something that the real estate industry, for example through the National Association of Realtors®, has put together through a series of courses or material that's specific to a particular line of thinking or particular type of customer. So, for example, you could have a CRS, which is a Certified Residential Specialist. So that's somebody who specializes in residential real estate. Or you have an SFR®, also known as a Short Sales and Foreclosure Resource. I'm an actual SFR®. I'm certified in short sales.

What the designation does for you as an agent, is it gives you the ability to market to your clients, to your prospects, and say, "I have this designation. Which means I have this specialization." Another one that I have is an e-PRO®, because I do a lot of online marketing. It's like anything else in your sales business; it's a marketing tool.

It's a way to communicate with your clients that you have an extra level of training in that specific category. So, if you're taking your CE, or your Continuing Education classes, to renew your license, why not use your electives to get a designation? It helps, and you're going to be able to specialize in a particular area of your own interest.

Chapter Two:

Mindset

Introduction

In this chapter, the focus is on mindset. How you see things and how you approach them. Both are very important not only in real estate, but also in life. The way you see things and how you think are going to affect the outcome of everything you do. The mindset you have will help determine whether you succeed or fail.

The real estate professionals in this chapter give you a wealth of advice about having the right mindset in real estate. You will learn a number of important lessons from them. Many of them also apply to life. You will:

Learn about being yourself, being honest, staying humble, and not having an ego.

Find out about being confident, managing your emotions, not taking things personally, and being charitable.

Also discover more about not comparing yourself to others and being motivated by big goals.

And, you will discover you always need to keep learning and to see failure not as a negative, but as an opportunity to learn even more.

You will also uncover business lessons. You will:

Find out about treating real estate like a job, treating your business like a business, and being consistent in your work.

Read about mastering one thing at a time and being more effective with your time.

You will also read about interacting with clients. You will:

Learn about understanding difficult clients and contributing to clients.

Read the lesson of not making interactions about yourself.

Also there is a reminder to ask for business.

That's just some of what you'll find out about having the right mindset for real estate. There are other lessons too. The point of them all comes back to the same idea:

How you see the world, affects the world you see. What you focus on expands.

If you want to see a good world in your business, you have to see it in the right way.

Treat Real Estate Like a Real Job

Mikki-Michelle Shuler-Gaul, Clarkston, Michigan

Mikki-Michelle Shuler-Gaul:

Really, just treat this like a job. It isn't a game, it isn't a vacation, and it isn't a hobby. It is a job, and if you treat it like a job, you will get paid, and you'll get paid well, regardless of your education, or your standing in life. You can rise to anything in this business if you just work at it like a job. If you're a hard worker, there's no reason you can't succeed.

Alex Saenger:

You know, Brian Buffini says, "In real estate, there's no ceiling. You can go as high as you want. There's also no floor though."

Meaning, if you don't put any effort into real estate, into the job of being a real estate agent, you could make nothing at all, or even lose money! But if you put in the effort, and if you put in the time, there's no telling how high you can take the work that you do and the business that you're growing.

In the work that you put into real estate, the results you get are directly proportional to how much effort you put into the business. So if you want to be a successful agent, put in the time.

Wait, Limiting Beliefs do What to My Business?

Susan Buchman, Albuquerque, New Mexico

Susan Buchman:

Having no limitations is important. I think taking the cap off of limitations, and limiting beliefs of being new and trying to compete with top agents or big teams is important. It's important not to limit myself.

I think that anything is possible, and finding the tools and reaching out is part of the reason I love Keller Williams. It's because of the tools that are available to us. Our market center is amazing at supporting our newer agents. Don't reinvent the wheel. I think finding the things, understanding that there's no limiting beliefs, and finding the tools to help you succeed are important.

Alex Saenger:

Limiting beliefs. What does that mean? Well, as a new agent, you think, "Well, if I could just do one transaction a month, I'd have 12 sales in a year." Well, what if you did one transaction a week? How about that? What would that look like? Or maybe, what about 100 transactions in a year? What about a thousand transactions in a year? Is that possible? Yes, it is.

But most people don't think about it that way. They think, "I'm only one person, and I can only do this thing, this one thing. This one little amount of stuff." While that's true, there's only so much you can do by yourself, it doesn't mean that you can't surround yourself with great people and great leverage that can allow you to achieve a much higher level of success.

Similarly, you might think, "Well, I'd like to be able to build my profit share, my passive income, through profit share at Keller Williams. If I recruit somebody, I might get $1,000 or $2,000. Really, what does that do for me?" But what if I told you it's not really that hard to get $20,000 or $30,000 dollars? There are even agents in our organization that make a million dollars a year just in profit share. Now, do you think that they have limiting beliefs? The answer is that they don't, because they understood that if they applied themselves, if they worked the system, if they worked the industry, if they worked their database, if they worked their lead generation, their limits could get blown right out of the water and they could achieve way more success than they ever imagined.

Getting past your limiting beliefs is probably one of the first steps in changing your mindset in being even more successful than you imagined.

Business and Your Lifestyle

Jessica Carter, Ann Arbor, Michigan

BUSINESS AND YOUR LIFESTYLE

Jessica Carter:

One issue is probably wanting to have more of a life and wanting to give up business sometimes. Whereas I used to go after everything that was coming my way, now I just want to have more of a life. If it's something that's going to spin my wheels, I've learned to let it go. I think letting go has really allowed me to grow.

Alex Saenger:

I love what Jessica's talking about here. Being selective and really fitting your business into the lifestyle that you want to have. You know, early in my career, when I first got started, I was just like Jessica. My attitude was, "I'm just going to take any deal I can get," because I was that hungry, even desperate. But as my business grew and as I became more comfortable and more confident in my own abilities, I realized I don't need to be a 24-hour agent. I can be the 9 to 5 agent. I can treat real estate like a job and not let it consume my life. I made a decision, and I decided, you know what, I'm going to work 9 to 5.

When I meet with my clients, it's going to be within these windows. I'll have some times where I can work late or maybe occasionally on a weekend I can do an open house, things like that. But what I realized was, people want to meet with you after hours because that's kind of what they expect of you as an agent. In my case, I have three kids. When I explain to them, "Look, I've got three kids and they've got a lot of activities in the evenings and on weekends, so I'm not really available then. But when I am available is Tuesday at 2 or Thursday at 3, which one works better for you?" When you couch it that way, and you present it to your client that way, guess what? If they have kids, they completely understand what you're talking about. And they take one of the options you give them, just like they will for an orthodontist appointment.

Let's face it, real estate is probably one of the biggest investments they're going to have in their life, whether they're selling or they're buying. It's going to matter a lot. They can take some time off to meet with you. That's the way I treat my business. Other people, like dual career agents, they only have time in the evenings and on weekends, and so that might be how they decide to run their business. All that matters is being yourself and being selective with whom you work with.

And by the way, if they don't fit into your lifestyle, it's okay. You can refer them to another agent that maybe is the opposite of you, and that will work too. You'll get a referral fee from them, and your client will be happy. You're going to be happy too, because you're not taking them out to see a house at a time that doesn't work for you and the way you want to run your business. Make sure that you fit your lifestyle with your schedule and be yourself.

Balance Your Life to Avoid Burnout

Roseanne Powell, Shelby Township, Michigan

Roseanne Powell:

100% balance. Make absolutely certain that no matter what you're doing, you are doing work, play, and balance. You've got to balance your life or else you're going to burn out in this business.

Alex Saenger:

You need to focus on balance. The fact of the matter is, having work life balance is extremely important not just in your personal life, but in terms of your health and your business. A healthy work life balance makes your business thrive because those connections that you make personally also impact your business and vice versa. Just remember, every time you say yes to something, you're saying no to something else. That has a direct impact on the balance you have between your life and your business.

Control Your Mornings, Control the Outcome of Your Day

Dan Burgess, Palo Alto, California

Dan Burgess:

Start with your daily habits. Start with your mornings. Control your mornings. Control the outcome of the beginning of each day, and you'll be super successful.

Alex Saenger:

Dan talks about your daily habits and controlling your morning. The morning is your most productive time of the day. It's the time, as a real estate agent, where you really want to spend your time prospecting. It's something that needs to happen every single day, and it's something that is most effective in the morning. Now, yes, you can say, "Oh people are heading to work, or they're eating their breakfast, or whatever." But the fact is, if you don't spend the time in the morning prospecting, you might not get it done at all that day. And if you don't get your prospecting done, you're not going to have any leads. And if you don't have any leads, you don't have any listings. And if you don't have any listings, you don't have any leverage. So, how you setup your time, how you time block, and how you spend your time in the morning is critically important to the success you have for the rest of the week, the rest of the month, and the rest of the year.

Plan Your Vacations Ahead of Time

Liza and Tina Vernazza, San Carlos, California

Tina Vernazza:

I think about being purposeful with my business, whereas before, it would just come.

Liza Vernazza:

Plan your vacations ahead of time.

Tina Vernazza:

Yes, exactly. Plan the vacations, number one, and then make your goals. Plan your business for the year, and then it just happens. You know, you work hard and it happens.

Liza Vernazza:

Well, we know that we're not going to spend all day and all week on our business, and there's not an unlimited amount of time, so we have to be more effective.

Tina Vernazza:

We're more purposeful with our time spent.

Liza Vernazza:

Because, there's a plan.

Tina Vernazza:

Yes, our time spent is more purposefully. We're not just lollygagging in the office. Because we have a plan.

Liza Vernazza:

No chit chat.

Tina Vernazza:

Yes. Yes, no chit chat. Exactly.

Alex Saenger:

There are a couple of things that they talked about in that back and forth interview. First, be very purposeful with your time. Make sure that you know how you're spending it. Maybe time block if you haven't done it already. It's something that comes up constantly.

But one thing that I really liked that they talked about, is plan your vacation ahead of time. So, at the beginning of the year, you're pulling out your calendar, you're figuring out when's summer vacation, when are the kids off. You're going ahead and marking it up on the calendar when you're not going to be working.

And you know what happens when you do that? It's when the business comes. Just to let you know, it's Murphy's Law. Whenever you're planning on going away, that's when the business is going to come. I see it every year!

So, plan your vacation, plan your training, and then whatever's left over, that's the time that you have to focus on your business. Now, I will tell you that we had July coming up, and July was the month where I decided to take my family to Europe, and to England actually. Sure enough, that's when all the business was coming. But what's great about it was, I could kind of plan my business around my trip. So, if somebody said, "Oh, I'm thinking about putting the house on the market," I could say, "That's fine. I can get everything done that I need to get done before I leave. My team can take over while I'm gone. Or you know what? Since I'm going to be gone, do you want to do this before I leave or do you want to do it when I come back?" I'm actually having that conversation months in advance because I already know when I'm going to be gone.

Having that plan in place is super important so that you can have clear communication with your clients, because they want you to. That's why they talk to you, right? It's why somebody was referred to you, they want you. But they also want to respect that you have a family and a life outside of business. They want to respect the fact that you're going to go on vacation. They want you to enjoy your trip. In fact, one of my clients said, "You know what, Alex, let's get this house sold so you have some spending cash on your vacation." I mean, what a great client to have to say something like that, right?

That's the kind of thing that you can do by being purposeful with your time. Planning ahead, putting vacation time on the calendar, and making sure that you set aside the time you need for 1) your family, for 2) your training, and 3) everything else that's going on in your life.

The Monthly Tasks That Make You a Business Professional

Liza Vernazza, San Carlos, California

Liza Vernazza:

Running my business like a business and keeping track of my profit and loss, my expenses, what's going on in my business, and the return on investment, and things like that. That's really changed the way I do business.

Alex Saenger:

As a business person you may have heard of a P&L (profit and loss statement), or ROI (return on investment). In real estate those same principles apply to your business, because it is a *business*. It's not a hobby. It's something that you're doing to make a profit. And in real estate one of the things that we look at when we make an investment is we want to make sure that if we're spending a dollar, we're getting four or five dollars back at least. If you're just exchanging one dollar for another dollar, meaning we "broke even," then what's the point of doing it, right?

When you're thinking about investing in marketing, or technology, or anything else that you're going to do, or people for that matter, you want to make sure that you're getting four to five times the return on your investment so that your profit and loss statement at the end of the year is on the profit side.

Stay Humble

Nathan Biggar, Tempe, Arizona

Nathan Biggar:

Stay humble. Clients don't like cocky real estate agents and there's too much of that out there. They don't really care what you do as long as they trust you, and they care what you do but they don't care what you've done necessarily. They care about themselves having the best experience possible and that they can trust you. So focus on those things.

Alex Saenger:

What Nathan's talking about is when you're spending time with your client, or for that matter, interacting with another agent on a transaction. In those situations, be careful not to be too prideful, or behave like somebody that's focused on being elitist, or condescending. Don't be too focused on your own reputation and not focused enough on the relationship that you have with your client, or the relationship that you're having with the other agent.

It's so important that the relationship with the other agent and with your client maintains a sense of responsibility to the transaction and to the fiduciary responsibility to your client; and for that matter, to collaboration with the other agent. You're not adversaries. You're not trying to one-up one another. Leave your ego at the door. You're trying to work together, to keep that transaction together, and to make a win-win for both the buyer and the seller.

So, when you're thinking about how to interact with people, don't make it about you. Make it about your client, make it about the relationship with the other agent, or even make it about the transaction, so that you can create a win-win for everyone involved in the transaction.

Be True to Who You Are

Cole Whisenhunt, Lubbock, Texas

Cole Whisenhunt:

The advice that I got was good, it was be yourself. You're going to learn different scripts, you're going to learn how to generate business, but at the core of that you have to be yourself. Whenever you take those scripts and the language in them and the point of all of them, it's for a purpose and there are different points within scripts and business conversations that you have to have. But you have to be yourself within that. You can take those scripts and make them your own. I think it's going to be dynamite. So don't get away from who you are because it's so natural, but at the same time you have to be very purposeful and driven, rather than entrepreneurial and just making things up. Follow your scripts and make them your own.

Alex Saenger:

So there are lots of ways to interpret what Cole is talking about. One way that I like to think about it is, be yourself. You know, you have your own personality. Of course, don't be rude or offend people, but be yourself. Be who you are. You'll never catch me wearing a tie. The only times I wear a tie are to a funeral or a wedding. Otherwise, you're going to find me in a polo shirt or a button-down shirt, maybe some khaki pants, some jeans, and shorts in the summer.

But the point is, that I'm going to be who I am, but I'm also going to be genuine. Yes, I'm going to learn my scripts and I'm going to deliver those in my style, but I'm still going to be genuine to who I am as a person. I feel that if I do that, the people that I'm interacting with, they're going to be much more comfortable with me. And let's face it, not everybody's going to like you, but some people will. And the people that do like you, those are the people you want to hang out with. And you know what? Those people that like you, they tend to be friends with other people that are like them. By the way, those happen to also be people who like people like you. It's amazing how you can actually build your business out by just focusing on people that you resonate with, by being natural, and being yourself.

Why Comparing Yourself to Others Doesn't Work

Alyson Hamel, Whitefish Bay, Wisconsin

Alyson Hamel:

Don't compare yourself to others. I did that right when I started, and it really put me down. So newer agents, never compare yourself to others, because everyone is at a different walk in their career, and you are who you are. God created you as you, so don't try to compare yourself to anyone else.

Alex Saenger:

Alyson is talking about what doesn't work – trying to compare yourself to other people. Now let's flip that onto the other side. Instead of figuring out how to compare yourself to other people, let's figure out what makes you unique compared to other people. That is the thing that people are most interested in.

Think about all the people you know. There are probably a couple of people that pop out in your mind as being unique for some reason. So take me for example. I've done a personality assessment. According to that assessment, I deliver ambitious results to my clients. But I'm also somebody that really tries to have a positive outreach with other people so that I can lift them up and I can help them with their real estate needs. This book is an example of that. That's one of the things that makes me unique as a person, as a business-owner, as somebody who is trying to find his way in life through real estate.

So ask yourself, what makes you unique? That's what you really need to focus on as a new agent, or even as an experienced agent that's been in the business for a while. Those things that make you unique are the things that you should embrace and make louder in your world. If you've enjoyed this book, then you know exactly what I'm talking about, because this book is a unique way that I am reaching out to you. And maybe, just maybe, when you know someone thinking about moving to the Washington, D.C. metro area, you will remember that great agent who wrote this book Real Agent Advice and send that referral to Alex Saenger. After all, he knows his stuff, right?

Love What You Do and Your Clients Will See It

Susan Salazar, Franklin, Tennessee

Susan Salazar:

Love what you do. If you love what you do it will show. It'll show to your clients. They'll see that you're happy doing your job. They'll see that you really enjoy what you do and you take care of them because it's not just a job for you. If they think that you love what you're doing and you're really helping them, they're going to want to refer you and have you take care of their family and friends too.

Alex Saenger:

Love what you do. You've got to be more of who you are, you've got to be genuine and authentic. And when you're doing that and you really are who you are with your clients and everyone around you, they're going to love you for who you are and the way you do business. So, if you want more clients and you want genuine relationships with really great referrals, be yourself, do a great job, and be enthusiastic about it.

Fail Fast to Grow as a Real Estate Agent

Maria Hurtado, Yuma, Arizona

Maria Hurtado:

Failure was a stepping stone to where I want to be. It's not a failure, it's just an experience. Learn from it. Get up, and move on.

Alex Saenger:

So as Maria states, failures are not failures. They're stepping stones to success. In fact, at Keller Williams, one of the things that we talk about a lot is "fail fast". It allows you to move on past the thing that's not working. You then can go on to the next step, on to the next thing that might be the breakthrough that you're looking for.

If you're afraid of failure, don't be. It happens to every single one of us and it's just a part of the journey to the success of your business.

Reasons to Take Ignite More Than Once

Jenney Szeto, Cambridge, Massachusetts

REASONS
TO TAKE IGNITE
MORE THAN ONCE

Jenney Szeto:

I think as a new agent, the best thing to do in the very beginning is to learn and absorb everything. I took Ignite twice already, even though I only joined in December. I took it first in November and then I took it again in December. I would say in the very beginning take Ignite. Do everything you can. The lead generation is very important, but just absorb everything and be a sponge.

Alex Saenger:

As a new agent or an agent maybe that hasn't done a lot of business, one of the things that every market center (every office) makes available to our employees, to our agents, is an Ignite class. Ignite (a 12 week intense program for new agents) is the thing that sets you on fire and lets you blaze into the marketplace really doing a lot of business. The classes are designed to teach you the fundamentals of real estate, the fundamentals of lead generation, and doing things like going and visiting 10 properties every week, having 10 conversations with people, writing handwritten notes, making those phone calls, and doing those scripts. All those things that you need to do to be successful.

Ignite is something you should look into if you're a new agent. Talk to your local Keller Williams office about what classes they have available that you might be able to take advantage of right now, even if you haven't joined yet. I guarantee you there's something there that they can share with you that you're going to find extremely valuable, and you might decide you like this, and you'd love to join the office.

If you want an introduction, let me know. I'm happy to help. Contact me at coffee@RealAgentAdvice.com and you and I can get to know one another. I can be your sponsor to help you change your life and implement all the advice found in these pages. I would be honored to help you unlock your full potential.

Why You Should Want to Learn Like You'll Live Forever

Dianna Kokoszka, Austin, Texas

Dianna Kokoszka:

An open mindset is so important. A fixed mindset is where you already think you know it. You don't want to learn, you don't ask questions and you definitely don't listen. You don't need to go to any classes because you already know it and therefore, you're not going to make it.

How do I think differently now because I've had a Breakthrough? I've had a lot of Breakthroughs. I don't think I think anything differently. I'm still learning-based. I want to learn like I'll live forever and live like I'll die tomorrow. The fact is, you never stop learning. So I don't know what would be different. I'm constantly asking questions of Gary Keller and other great people.

When you are in a learning-based mode, you're the one that's always asking the questions and you're the one that always controls the conversation.

Alex Saenger:

Dianna's talking about being learning-based. Ask lots of questions because those questions are going to be the things that get you the answers that you need to propel your business and your life forward. After all, Dianna doesn't just know everything, right? She talks about how she asks questions of Gary Keller and some of the other people in her life because, regardless of what part of her career she's in, she's going to want to propel herself forward. As a CEO, you would think, well they know everything. But even CEOs like Dianna need to ask questions of other people so that they can propel their businesses forward.

How Teaching Others Helps You to Grow

Sujatha Bhaskara, Morganville, New Jersey

Sujatha Bhaskara:

I think you grow while you teach. I think that's great. Take every moment that you have, and every opportunity that you have, to coach someone that is looking to be where you are today. I think that's tremendously fulfilling and it also helps you grow. When you speak about a topic you don't realize how much you know about it until you start teaching it to someone else.

Alex Saenger:

What Sujatha's talking about, is coaching other people. This is not necessarily for the new agents, it's more for the experienced agents, or teaching about something where you have skills. Maybe you know a lot about Facebook or Instagram or Twitter, something like that, and somebody else is struggling with that.

Take the opportunity to explain to them how they can leverage what you've learned. Teach them the things that they need to know. What you'll find is, as you teach, you become better at the thing that you're teaching. Because of this, in some respects, the things that you should be focused on teaching, are the things that you, despite having an understanding of, need help with. As you prepare to teach the material to someone else, you, yourself, will gain a better understanding of it.

In fact, one of the things at Keller Williams that we do, is we have a course called Ignite. It's where a lot of new agents come in and they learn the business from experienced agents. And one of the things that I challenge myself with, is teaching a class where I myself need work.

So, for example, if I need to work on my listing presentation, I might teach a class on listings or listing presentations. It forces me to go through my process and teach my process to those other students.

It then also makes me realize what things I could improve upon, and sometimes they'll have feedback for me that allows me to actually improve what I'm teaching.

The Joy of Helping People Find a Home

Dee Rolig, Shawnee, Kansas

THE JOY OF HELPING PEOPLE FIND A HOME

Dee Rolig:

Helping people brings you the best joy of your life. I love helping first time home buyers. I love, well, most situations. It's a happy situation whether people are buying or selling. It's just fun to be in an intimate part of their life and it brings me a lot of joy.

Alex Saenger:

To me, when you think about real estate, often people focus on the business. When you take a step back, you realize you really are helping people with one of the biggest decisions of their lives. Where they're going to live, where they're going to have a family, and where they're going to raise their children. When you really start to understand and think about the impact that you have on somebody's life, to be such an important part of that, it's actually a privilege to be honored to be selected to help that person. Take a minute to step back and think about the big picture of what you're actually doing to help somebody in their life through your job and through real estate.

The Giver

Laurie Satushek, Bellingham, Washington

Laurie Satushek:

I guess my success comes from the idea that I come from contribution. Before I was in real estate, I was a teacher for 22 years. My heart has always been to help people. I'm a giver, and people know that. They trust me. They know that I have their best interests in mind. People know that. They can tell.

Alex Saenger:

Laurie's a giver. A lot of us, as real estate agents, we are. We're just givers. We love giving clients our best. We love contributing to our communities. We love sharing. It's in our nature. When you come from a place of contribution, you're giving to your community. You're giving to your loved ones. You're giving to your friends. You're giving to people you've just met. Why? Because you are a giver. You are a generous person.

But here's the thing, it's important to be able to do that, but it's also important to make sure that at some point in the conversation, you are asking for business in return. Now, I'm not saying that you should lead with that. I'm not saying that you should start that as part of the conversation every time you have a conversation with somebody. Being generous, giving, is wonderful, but you're not in real estate to just give. You're not a philanthropic business that is basically giving everybody else what you have and leaving nothing for yourself and your family.

Asking for business is one of the most important parts of real estate that a lot of people overlook, so be sure to remind people that you are in real estate and that you're always available for any referrals that they might want to send you.

What Makes Someone Difficult

Catherine Kelly, Morristown, New Jersey

WHAT MAKES SOMEONE DIFFICULT

Catherine Kelly:

I love people. Being a real estate agent gives you an opportunity to meet incredible people. People say "Oh, difficult clients." I don't believe in difficult clients, because people are people and everybody has their needs. They're all looking out for what they want in life. You're being given an opportunity to serve people in a fantastic way to help them with the largest investment that they're probably ever going to make in their life, and you're going to be a part of that and helping them. That's what I think is so fantastic about being in real estate.

Alex Saenger:

Serving your clients is extremely important and having difficult clients, it's quite frankly, just part of the job. It's important to understand though, that somebody might be difficult not because they're difficult but because they're going through something. It's interesting, because when you give a client a call and maybe they snap at you or do something like that, you don't know what's really going on with them. You have to remember not to take it personally.

Think about it, there are times, and days, where you go through things maybe at home or at work or something else and you're talking to somebody that's not related to that subject. They don't know that you just had a bad day. Maybe you just had a loved one that passed away and you're dealing with it, you're grieving and you're frustrated. Or maybe you just had a car accident and they're calling you 10 minutes after you got to work and you just had to go through all of that.

There are a lot of different reasons why people have difficult times in their lives. We don't know where they are mentally and what happened in their day that brought them to that moment in your interaction. When you think about a difficult client, think "You know what? Maybe there's something going on in their life that I don't know about. What can I do? What I can bring to the conversation to be positive? To be genuine. To smile."

How Honest Should You be With Your Clients?

Cole Whisenhunt, Lubbock, Texas

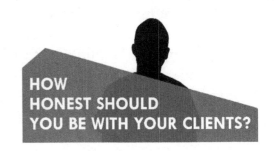

HOW HONEST SHOULD YOU BE WITH YOUR CLIENTS?

Cole Whisenhunt:

Be honest when it's tough and when it's easy. There's that part of the conversation where you ask, "How honest do you want me to be on the scale of one to ten?" I'm always hoping they say ten. If they don't, I just tell them, "Naturally, I'm a ten, and I want to be honest with you at all times."

Again, whether that's tough and I've got to have a tough conversation, whether it's about an appraisal or we need to have a price improvement, or it's easy, full price, first day on the market and get under contract, either way I'm going to be honest about the transaction.

Alex Saenger:

What Cole's talking about, is really being you, and being authentic. That means being honest with your customers and your clients and making sure they get all the information that they need. The question he asked is, "On a scale from one to ten, when it comes to tough questions, how frank and honest do you want me to be with you?" Most of the time I get people that say, "Well, I want you to be a ten. I don't want you to lie to me, right? Who wants to be lied to, right?"

When I give my listing presentation, my philosophy is actually written right in there. And my philosophy is really one that tells them, "My job is to tell you the truth. My job is to educate you through the process whether you're buying or you're selling a home. And it really doesn't matter to me whether you buy, sell, rent or invest. What matters to me is that you're getting the advice that you need to make the best decision for you and your family. After all, that's the way you want to be treated, right?" Well, me too. And that's the way I'm going to treat my clients. I know if I do that, then ultimately they're going to get the best service, and in the end, they're going to get exactly what they want. They're going to have a great experience and more than likely they're actually going to send me a referral more easily and more readily than had I done something different than that.

You Know What You Know

Mercedes French, Huntington Beach, California

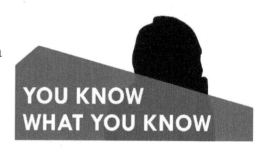

Mercedes French:

You don't know what you don't know. There's so much information out there, especially with all the technology that's come into play recently. It really can be overwhelming. You really need to figure out what it is that you want to do, where your passion is, what your niche is going to be. Then just go after that hard. Find out the tools that are going to help you get there.

Alex Saenger:

So you know what you know, you know what you don't know, right? I've always said this. Whenever I'm teaching, whenever I'm with a client, "You know what you know. You know what you don't know." Don't try to blow smoke at them and tell them something that isn't true.

One thing that I learned from Joe Niego from Buffini and Company was this whole concept of, "Well, let me double check". It implies that you have an idea of what it is, but you want to verify it before you give an answer.

Another perspective on this particular topic are the videos that this book is based on. The interviews that I've done for you, all of these different people that you're meeting through this book, these are all interviews that I made because, quite frankly, there's a lot that I didn't know. And through this process of interviewing for the videos I, myself, learned a lot about what all these wonderful agents were talking about, and I wanted to share that with you.

Don't be afraid to admit that you don't know everything. You can always "double check" on things if you're not quite sure. You can use tools like this book to get educated on different subjects and different topics. You can use this as a springboard to go investigate other things that you might be interested in. After all, this book is not supposed to be a complete source of information, but rather a source of insight and inspiration.

T.O.T.O.T.

Jayson Stone, Upper Marlboro, Maryland

Jayson Stone:

New Year's Day is getting ready to come. On that date, everyone will be at the same starting line. On January 1st, when the clock hits midnight, everyone will have sold zero homes in that year. It's an equal playing field and equal ground. The most important thing that matters to success on executing the game plan for the new year is Time-On-Task-Over-Time (TOTOT), as it applies to your lead generation activities. Are you willing to stay committed to your lead generation plan? Which is, time blocking for lead generation three hours or more per day.

Commitment means staying loyal to what you said you were going to do long after the mood that set it in has left you. That is what Time-On-Task-Over-Time represents. And the biggest thing that has empowered me, in the six years that I've now been in real estate, to remain loyal, to remain committed to those Time-On-Task-Over-Time activities, is being empowered by a big "Why?"

When I got into real estate, I had three main objectives after graduating college. I wanted to 1) get married to my then girlfriend, now wife, 2) buy a house, and I wanted to 3) start a family. When you have your big "Why" clearly defined, when the why is clear, you can endure any "how". And that's what commitment allows you to do when you remain loyal to Time-On-Task-Over-Time.

Alex Saenger:

So, as you can tell, Time-On-Task-Over-Time is really about consistency. Having a plan and making sure it's all grounded in a big "why". Now, as you may know, Simon Sinek wrote a great book about how to define your why. If you don't have a big "why," I suggest you start here and create your big "why". Remember, Gary Keller's "The ONE Thing" also ties into that as well.

So make sure you have your big "why." Stay consistent. Have a plan. And spend your Time-On-Task-Over-Time. You'll be successful before you know it. Have a great new year!

How the Business has Made Me a Better Mom

Angie Fucigna

Angie Fucigna:

I have a daughter who's almost 12, and the way that I parent my child, and teach her how to set goals, which I do for myself, has been impacted by the business. It's taught me to be a better mom. I'm bringing up a strong young lady. It's the best gift in the world.

Alex Saenger:

What's wonderful about real estate is that we can take a lot of the experiences that we have running our businesses and helping our clients, and implement those in our personal lives. Angie talks about setting goals with her daughter. That's a wonderful thing to do, and it's something that everybody should learn at a very young age. I know I didn't set goals when I was very young, but now in my business I do.

For example, with my kids, with my daughters, I actually implemented showing them how to plan out a project so that they can understand what it is going to take to get from beginning to end, and actually execute on that. Just like I would execute on one of my projects, like maybe putting a house on the market. That's a project that has a start, and it has an end. There are lots of steps in between. What are those steps? How long is it going to take? Whom am I going to need to get involved with that project?

So that's something that you can actually do to let your family know, let your kids know, how to interact with the world. How to plan. How to set goals, and all kinds of things. So keep in mind, real estate is not just a job. It's a way to experience life and share it with your family.

(By the way, the project I had my kids plan out was their Girl Scouts Silver and Gold Awards. College is approaching fast, and they can use any edge they can get!)

What You Focus on Expands

Michele Mamo, Cincinnati, Ohio

Michele Mamo:

"I'm going to raise my price point." And what you think about and focus on expands. So we focused on a higher price point. I already knew as an agent, how to get business and how to lead generate, but to focus on a higher price point was something different. They say, "You know, I don't want to do this price point, this is what I'm good at." I come up with strategies for that. We started doing staging. We were very, very conscious of really focusing on customer service at a high level and that really worked for us.

Alex Saenger:

Put your energy in your business, and in your day, and in your life, and it will expand. For example, the Real Agent Advice video series this book is based on. I communicate with people through that medium. That medium allows me to expand my referral business because viewers are going to send me referrals for Washington, D.C.

But we've taken it another step and created this book. This book is an accompaniment to The Millionaire Real Estate Agent by Gary Keller. We put it out. We got it out to you. It wasn't very expensive for you. We didn't make it expensive. In it, you can find information from the video series and different categories. You are able to research what you want. Find the information, go back and watch the video, and share with a friend. All in an effort to, give back to you before I ask you for a referral.

We did not start out with all this as a goal. Real Agent Advice started off because I wanted to find out, why do people come to Keller Williams? And, during the process, during that journey, I discovered that there was so much great content that I was getting from all these interviews, from all these agents from across the nation. When I culled this information, I said, "Wow! You know what? If we just had little sound bites once a day, to give us inspiration, to kind of get going for the day, how cool would that be?"

So, we wound up taking what was "finding out why people come to KW," and we wound up turning it into Real Agent Advice. And now it's a book that can provide you with valuable information and you can share it with a friend. Maybe share it with somebody who isn't part of KW. Or, for that matter, with someone who's thinking about getting into real estate.

By the way, you can share the videos in the series with anybody you want. Take the link, www.RealAgentAdvice.com, and put it up on Facebook, and add some subscribers. More importantly, just learn from them. Take the advice that we're sharing in this book and through the videos. We're giving you the opportunity to learn from experts that have been there before you.

Oh, and by the way, I would love a referral from you for the Washington, D.C., MD or VA areas! Just saying …

Focus on the One Thing

Wendy Papasan, Austin, Texas and Kymber
Menkiti, Washington, D.C.

Wendy Papasan:

If you want to get good at something, you need to do it over and over and over.
Let me give you an example. I have a woman who is Rookie of the Year in Austin,
not just for Keller Williams, but for the whole city of Austin, which is a very
competitive place. Her thing that year, all she did was open houses. She ended up
selling over ten million dollars of real estate that first year, which is really
impressive. What's amazing about the story though, is she did not get her first
buyer until the 35th open house. 35th! And people are like, "I'm not good at open
houses." Okay, well you're bad at it, so you have to get good at something. You
have to have mastery over it. The way you do that is to focus on the one thing.

Kymber Menkiti:

Don't chase all the rabbits. You've got to really identify and stick to that. In the
consistency of what your activity is, in that sort of geometric progression, a lot of
people stop right when they're getting ready to hit the curve, right? It's a gradual
incentive. So you're doing the activity and doing the activity, and you're ready to
give up on the 34th open house, and the first buyer is at the 35th. So identifying
what is that activity, and being committed to a 12-month cycle of staying with that
activity to see it through is important.

Wendy Papasan:

That's true.

Kymber Menkiti:

Invest in yourself, not in a magic potion.

Alex Saenger:

There is a book called The ONE Thing written by Gary Keller and Jay Papasan. The ONE Thing really focuses on what's the one thing that you can do such that by doing it everything else becomes unnecessary or easier. That's kind of a synopsis of what the idea behind the book is.

In the example that Wendy gave, she talked about the agent who focused on open houses. That was her one thing. I'm going to generate business from open houses. Now, if you think about it, Kymber touched on the idea of gradual and then all of a sudden. So, the person that's doing the open houses does a bunch of open houses and then hits the 34th. That person is really not having success and then all of a sudden after 34, BOOM, business skyrockets. That is the idea behind gradual and then all of a sudden. People always ask, "Where'd that person come from? They came out of nowhere." Well, no, the person has been doing a lot of work, it's just you didn't notice it.

Another example is when you see ducks on the surface of the water. The ducks are just sort of gliding on the surface of the water. They're just smoothly working their way across the pond or across the lake. Well, what you don't see, is underneath the water their feet are kicking a million miles an hour just to make them move across the water. That's the same idea here. You have to put in all this work to finally get that result that you're looking for.

If you're someone who's thinking about real estate and you're scattered and all over the place, you're kind of like that busy bee or squirrel. Stop. Get focused. Do the one thing that's going to make you successful. Dive in deep, and until you become a master at that one thing, you shouldn't really focus on doing other things.

When you do that, you'll realize that over time you'll improve gradually, and then all of a sudden the results will wind up coming from the activity that you do to get to the result that you're looking for.

La Confianza es Muy Importante

Roberto Linares Cantillo, Santa Ana Usaquén, Bogotá, Colombia

Roberto Linares Cantillo:

Confidence. Confidence. We like to serve our clients. We focus on confidence for them.

Alex Saenger:

So, confidence. What does confidence really mean? What does it portray to the person that you're interacting with?

If I'm talking to people who are confident, I think that they're knowledgeable. I think that they're trustworthy.

Think about this. If you were shy or hesitant and you were kind of backing away from the conversation, who then is in control of the conversation? Who then is in control of the negotiation? Who then has the upper hand, or is trustworthy?

Make sure that when you go into a situation, you are confident about what you know. You know what you know and you know what you don't know. Sound familiar? Don't fake the rest of it. Just tell them what you know and tell them if you don't know, "You know what, let me double check on that."

Being Confident in Your Own Resourcefulness

Dee Rolig, Shawnee, Kansas

Dee Rolig:

I think that you can't let a lack of confidence get you down because there's always someone there to help you. You're not going to know all the answers, but you just have to know where to go to get them.

Alex Saenger:

What's wonderful about confidence is, you know what you know and you know what you don't know. Ultimately, knowing whom to go to is one of the most important things that you can have in your arsenal of tools. Meaning, if you need a photography expert, you're going to find a photographer. Maybe you even have one on staff, and that's the person you're going to go to for photography. If you need a home staging expert, you're going to have that person that you can go to. If somebody says, "Well, should I use this color or that color? Should I keep the blinds or get rid of the blinds?" If you don't know or are unsure, your response should be, "You know what? I'm not sure, but let me get my professional advisor on that particular topic to come in and answer those types of questions for us."

You don't have to know everything, but you do have to be confident about the resources you have available to you that can answer the questions that your clients have. Make sure you build a team of real estate professionals outside of real estate. These are people like contractors, photographers, marketing specialists, finance people, and so on. Build a team of people around you, so that when you get those questions that you're uncomfortable answering, you can say, "You know what? I've got somebody that's perfect to answer that question. Let's get them involved."

Ask for Help

Ryan McHugh, Boca Raton, Florida

Ryan McHugh:

I learned, that if we put the idea that we have to do everything ourselves behind us and we actually ask for help, we can usually achieve anything that we want. I was a big believer of, "I have to do it all", especially in the beginning of being a team leader. Once I stepped back, asked for help, and realized that our company allows us to ask for help, 100 people lined up to help me in 15 minutes. That was pretty amazing.

Alex Saenger:

So, there are a couple of situations, recently, where I've had to ask for help. It wasn't that I had to, but it was going to make my life a whole lot easier, and make the lives of everybody around me a whole lot easier. One example? As some of you may know, I sponsor a networking event at Mega Camp and at Family Reunion. Those are events where I've got about 300 or 350 people showing up, and at the last event that I had, I was the only one leading it, and I was concerned because that's a lot of people showing up all at the same time. I reached out to my team leader and said, "Hey, are you going to be there?" She said, "Yes." I said, "I could really use some help." She responded, "I'd be glad to help." And she came, she enjoyed herself, she had a great time, and she got to meet some people herself.

Similarly, I had an investment seminar that happened last month. When I was getting ready to do the investment seminar, I realized, "Oh, we only have five packets left and we need another 25 packets because we have 30 people registered." I went over to my market center administrator and just asked, "Hey, can you just make me some copies of these really quick while I get things started?" Sure enough, she got it done, and when she came in, she didn't just bring them to me, she actually passed them out to all the people that needed them.

Asking for help is a great way for you to just stay on track, stay on top of things, and make sure that you're leveraging the people around you because, guess what? At some point, they're going to need help, and they're going to ask you too.

Enlarging Your Vision to Include the Needs of Your Team Members

John Pace, Richmond, Virginia

John Pace:

I'm not following my profit and loss statements like I need to as a business owner. In fact, I realized that three days ago, prepping for a class. I sent my coach a message saying, "We've got to talk about profit and loss on Monday."

I'm not thinking big enough, is probably the next biggest one. One of my favorite quotes from Gary Keller is, "You've got to make sure your world is big enough to incorporate the lives and the people in your team's world." And so I've been really trying to stretch what do they want, and then, how I can build my world to encompass theirs so they never leave my business. So I need to constantly be thinking of what is the next thing I need to be doing so that my team can get what they want. And that extends to me getting what I want because I'm hoping they get where they want to go.

Alex Saenger:

So I've heard this concept before. Gary Keller talks about it. Other successful real estate teams talk about this concept of building a world, building a business, and building an environment that's big enough so that your team never wants to leave. Ultimately, it's about making a vision where they can see themselves growing into a different position within the organization, wherever they can imagine themselves growing into.

Ultimately, when you attract talent and you find people that are a perfect fit for your team, you want to give them the ability to grow into positions that they want for the rest of their lives. It's not an easy task to do and you can't do it as a solo agent. You have to do it as a team member or a team leader. And, if you're somebody that's thinking about joining a team, you need to make sure you find an agent that has a team and has a vision that's big enough that you can grow your business.

One of the things that I'm doing with my team, is identifying investment opportunities that everyone can get involved in. Because I don't just want my team to be successful in real estate, I also want to encourage wealth building so that they can build their futures for their families. Making sure that you have a big enough vision and big enough world that your team will grow into, is what he's talking about. And it's something that you should be thinking about for yourself, whether you're a team leader, building a team, or you're thinking about joining a team.

Where do You Focus Your Mind?

Leo Robles, Corona, California

Leo Robles:

I would heavily, heavily invest in my, rather your, mindset. Mindset is everything. It's about 80% of everything we do. Why a mindset? Because you have to learn how to manage your emotions. Your emotions are everything. On a transaction, when you're dealing with clients, you know every single thing that you're doing. It's all about managing emotions, so really invest in mindset. One of the books that really impacted my life was Unlimited Power by Tony Robbins. I read that book at 16, so I would definitely read it every day.

Alex Saenger:

Leo's talking about mindset. Where do you focus your mind? What place are you in emotionally, physically, and mentally, when it comes to actually interacting with your clients? I actually want to talk a little bit about something related to that but also not. Leo mentioned the book, Unlimited Power by Tony Robbins. Now, I want everyone reading this to understand, that what we're trying to do with this book, is not give you in-depth content and a full breadth of everything that you want to know. We're trying to remind you of different things every day that you can use to inspire your day.

In this interview we're focusing on mindset, and we're giving you the path to a book that you can read. Similarly, lots of the other interviews are going to give you a path to some other place where you can get more in-depth information. These interviews are designed to inspire you to go find that information and kick start your day so that you have a path and a direction. So that if you don't have the right mindset, we can help you get there.

Why You Should Keep Your Mind Free of Negative Thoughts

Gina Padro, Garden City, New York

WHY YOU
SHOULD KEEP
YOUR MIND FREE OF
NEGATIVE THOUGHTS

Gina Padro:

I removed negative thoughts from my life. There's no longer the situation that the business is running me. I'm running the business. I don't let people treat me the way I don't want them to treat me. I have just seen a tremendous amount of growth. The third time going through BOLD, KW MAPS Coaching, and all of these things has completely changed my mindset which has brought me to a completely new level in my business.

You just embrace it. You decide that I'm no longer going to continue this path. I am taking that path, and that path is positively, not negatively, growing with a positive mindset.

Alex Saenger:

What Gina's talking about is understanding your mindset. The narrative that you have in your mind is what shows up in reality. Having a positive attitude toward how you're going to run your business, engage with your clients, and manage your time is important for you having a successful business.

You're the one that determines how your time is spent and managed, not your clients. Many agents get that confused. They feel like, "I have to go rush out and take care of my client. I have to do it." Right? No, you don't have to stretch your time. They have to follow your process and they're going to appreciate that they're following your process and respecting your time, just as you're respecting theirs.

In addition to this, it is important not to take business personally. It can be easy to develop negative thoughts if you see things that don't go the way you want as being directed toward you.

So make sure you have a great mindset. Make sure you put the narrative that you want in your mind. Then go do your business and be prosperous.

The Practice of Generosity

JoAnn Callaway, Scottsdale, Arizona

JoAnn Callaway:

Always give, because you cannot give it away. Everything you do for someone else, every time you help another agent, every time you help a client, you are fulfilled a thousand times over, so you can't give it away.

Alex Saenger:

You should always look to help others. Always look to give your information and your insight to others by helping them. When you help someone else, it takes nothing from you, but it gives so much to them. To their life. To their person. To their business. Be a giver. Your generosity is the thing that's actually going to wind up helping you in the end get more business.

Why Keller Williams is the Place for Charitable Endeavors

Barbara Best, Toronto, Ontario, Canada

Barbara Best:

Kenny Klaus, I thought his ideas of bringing charity to his farm area were great. He does a branded paper bag for the food drive. I'm going to start implementing some of the ideas that he did from a charitable perspective and giving back to the community instead of just reinvesting in my business. I want to reinvest in my community and really be more of value to them. That was a big aha for me.

Alex Saenger:

There are a couple of things that make Keller Williams unique. One, we have different conferences across the nation where a bunch of us get together and share ideas. That's actually what Barbara's talking about. She learned something at one of the meetings that she went to at one of our big conventions called Family Reunion. Now, in this case, she's talking about donating, giving back to the community. She's talking about getting paper bags, collecting food, and bringing those donations to the food bank. This is something you can get your kids and your whole community involved in, and really just be a sponsor and a beacon for giving back.

In fact, at Keller Williams, another thing that makes us unique is Red Day, which stands for renew, energize, and donate. It's where the entire company shuts down and over 150,000 agents from across the nation plus their staff go and contribute to the community through donating their time, energy, effort, and money. It's a way for all of us to give back.

In fact, at this year's Red Day, we assembled dressers because it's actually one of the biggest needs they have at A Wider Circle. Our office actually purchased 10 dressers to bring to A Wider Circle for Red Day and we put them together so people can take them home.

If that's something that you'd like to be a part of, make sure you get in touch with your local Keller Williams office. And if you're at a Keller Williams office, make sure you talk to a Culture Committee member because they're going to be able to help you figure out what's going to happen next year for Red Day and how you can be involved.

Chapter Three:

Networking

Introduction

"Who you know." You've heard that expression before. It's networking. It's how you get a job. It's how you get business. It's how you get opportunity. It does lead to some questions though:

With whom can you network? Where can you meet them? How do you interact with them?

Don't worry. The real estate professionals in this chapter give you the advice you need to help you answer those questions, and get you motivated to do some networking.

With whom can you network?

In this chapter, you'll learn that you can network with other real estate agents. They could be agents in your office, the other agent in a deal, agents in other areas, entry level agents (particularly if you are one), more successful agents and just other agents generally. Some of these agents might turn out to be mentors for you and some of them might be successful people you can see as role models.

You'll also learn that you can network with home related businesses, especially those in the area you serve. These businesses could be contractors, painters, carpet layers, landscapers, plumbers, electricians or any other professional a home owner might need. You'll learn about the importance of being a resource for your community in this regard.

Additionally, you'll learn about networking with past clients and your friends. And you'll learn that it's all right for you to remind your friends that you're in real estate and you are available for their referrals.

Where can you meet them?

There are lots of ways that you can get in touch with the people you can network with. You'll learn that you can meet them at real estate events, like conferences. You can also meet them through networking groups and social media. In regards to social media, you'll learn about the importance of being real when using it and how you can use it to reach millennials.

How do you interact with them?

In this chapter you'll learn about the importance of networking constantly and of telling someone every day that you're in real estate. You'll learn about asking other agents questions to learn and about telling stories when you communicate. You'll gain an understanding of the importance of relationships, and how relationships can either start from a place of trust or a place of real estate.

Remember, networking is an important part of your business. It is how you interact with so many of the people around you. It is an important tool that can lead to referrals. This chapter will give you a start in learning about networking.

Don't be Afraid of Self Promotion

Dana Hollish-Hill, Washington, D.C.

Dana Hollish-Hill:

I think the easiest thing you can do is, every day, tell someone that you're in the real estate business. You can be at the gas station or at the soccer field. You can say, "Oh my, I have to go. I have to go sell some houses." I think you shouldn't have to always say the market's great. Real estate is great. You can say, "Wow, I don't have any listings right now, and I'd really love one if you know anyone who's selling their house?" It doesn't always have to be positive. It can be really honest and I think people appreciate it and help you out more if you do that.

Alex Saenger:

So what Dana's talking about is making sure that you're present and you're letting people know that you're in the real estate business. Talking about the fact that you are in the business and promoting yourself is one of the things we have to do. Sometimes it's really uncomfortable to promote yourself. The fact of the matter is, if we don't do it, who will? You can't rely on everybody else out there to give you referrals and to be your songbird. You have to make sure that you yourself are telling people constantly that you're in real estate.

The human mind only has the capacity to hold the names of two real estate agents. You want to make sure that you're one of those two. The way to do that is to consistently tell people you're in real estate.

Why You Need to Remind Your Friends That You're a Real Estate Agent

Deb Ritter, Glen Ellyn, Illinois

Deb Ritter:

Really put yourself out there. Let your friends know you're in real estate, because you're in real estate and that's awesome. It doesn't have to be a weird conversation. Just be natural and call them. They love you, they just want to know what you're doing. And even though they love you, they may not always remember. So just remind them in a nice way.

Alex Saenger:

A lot of people feel awkward about talking to people about real estate. They think, "They're my friends, they're the people I hang out with. I don't really want to, you know, mix business and pleasure." The fact of the matter is that real estate is a very personal business. It is something where you're going to be talking to your friends and helping the move.

It's okay. It's okay to get in touch with them and just let them know, in a nonthreatening way, that you're in real estate. You have to keep reminding them because they are not thinking of you that way. They're thinking of you as a friend, or as somebody that they know from school or from soccer or from whatever you might be involved in.

One of the ways I remind people I'm in real estate, is actually by wearing a logo on my shirt. So I don't have to bring it up, they bring it up. When I'm standing at a soccer practice or a volleyball practice, they're going to say, "Oh that's right, you're in real estate. Hey Alex, how's the market?" "Well that depends. Are you thinking about buying, selling, renting, or investing?" "Well, I'm not actually asking for myself, my sister is thinking about moving in California." "Really? Great, well does she have an agent because I'd love to give her a referral from somebody like you?"

So it's a way for you to get in touch with people and talk to them. Your logo on

115

your shirt or maybe a name badge or for that matter if you're just having a conversation, and right at the end, do the Columbo thing. "Oh by the way, do you know anyone right now that's thinking about buying or selling real estate? I'm looking for a great seller right now. Do you know anybody?" They're going to say, "You know what, I don't right now, but I'll keep you in mind." "Well great, thanks for taking a minute to think about that."

So those are the types of interactions you can have with your clients and with your friends to remind them that you're in real estate without being too threatening.

Nurture Relationships and Watch Clients Sing Your Praises

Angie Smart, Gainesville, Georgia

Angie Smart:

I wish somebody would have told me to really keep in touch with, not only people that I know from my sphere, but all my past clients. I think it is business changing. I mean, these are people that know you and love you, so they are your best referral people. They're going to tell all their friends and family and everybody that they loved you because you're so awesome. It's your best referral source.

Alex Saenger:

Angie talks about focusing on the people in your sphere that know you and love you the best. Those are the people that understand what value you bring to the perspective referrals that they're going to give you. They're your most vocal song birds. They're the people that actually will send you more business than anybody else. So make sure you nurture those relationships with them from a business perspective. Because, not only do we want them to know you and love you, but we want them thinking about you when it comes to real estate. So make sure that you get in touch with them. Have your 36 touch (a systematic plan to connect with people in your database 36 times a year), and make sure you're including those people in those touches. Make sure you're calling them at least once a quarter to talk about real estate. Make sure that you nurture those relationships.

Connect With Agents

Dee Rolig, Shawnee, Kansas

Dee Rolig:

It's really important to be connected with other agents. It's a career where, especially if you're a single agent, you can feel isolated at times, but there's always somebody out there going through the same thing you're going through. It's important to have those relationships and come to things like Family Reunion and it's just a wealth of information.

Alex Saenger:

Dee's talking about not isolating yourself. Don't be one of those agents that's at home trying to work from home and do everything there. Get into the office, get around other people, get around other agents that are doing more business than you are and learn from them.

We recently had a Regional Mastermind here in the Washington, D.C. metro area, and the Rookie of the Year came up on stage. They asked him, "What is it that made you this year's Rookie of the Year? You didn't really know anybody in real estate or anything like that." He said, that he came into the office every day and he brought one question to agents that had more experience than he had. Every time he asked a question he would learn something. He would then take something of value from the conversation and bring that to the next person that he talked to. He would say, "By the way, I just learned this. Is there something that you can teach me?"

He came from a place of contribution, and he didn't isolate himself sitting at home, which many agents do. He decided, "Let me be proactive and get involved and get in front of other agents, people that are doing way more business than I do, and let me learn from them." That's something that I took away from that particular Mastermind. Everybody has something to contribute and you can't contribute if you're at home. Make sure you're in the office, you're connecting with other agents, you're networking with them, and you're learning from each other.

Network Constantly to Connect With Buyers and Sellers

Greg Pedone, Los Gatos, California

Greg Pedone:

Make sure you network constantly. Go out there, go to different cities, go to different events and meet other agents and be a referral source for them and for the needs of our buyers and sellers.

Alex Saenger:

One of the things that you'll notice about the interviews that I have in the Real Agent Advice video series and in this book, is that they are with a variety of different people. The idea behind that was for me to actually network with other agents at events that brought agents from across the nation, and across the world, together so that I could bring you this great content. But in doing so, I built relationships with each one of those agents, just like I'm building with you right now. This is a way to network, by getting involved. Go to different events in your local community. Get involved in broker events. Get involved in regional events, or national events, like Keller Williams Mega Camp or Keller Williams Family Reunion. These are great places to meet tons of people. Keller Williams has over 160,000 agents. There are probably agents who are looking to send a referral into your neck of the woods right now, but they don't know about you because they didn't network with you … yet!

Network With Other Entry Level Agents

Joanne Curtin, Roswell, Georgia

Joanne Curtin:

I wish I would have networked more with some of the rookies of the year. That's something that I think I could have done better. I should've been involved a little bit more with young professionals groups.

That really would've made some lasting deep relationships that could really help my business today.

Alex Saenger:

When you first get into business, you are kind of graduating with a class of other like-minded real estate agents. People that are just getting started. Those relationships you have, just like when you were back in high school, are relationships that you want to maintain throughout your career.

Being able to connect and network with those other agents, having them show their clients your listings, or masterminding with them to come up with new ideas or breakthrough ideas on how you can actually attack the market, attack your business, attack negotiations, attack anything, is really important. So make sure you network and you build relationships with other agents. They're one of the most overlooked resources that we have available to us as real estate professionals.

Real Life Referral Success Story

Michele Youngblood, Chesterfield, Michigan

REAL LIFE REFERRAL SUCCESS STORY

Michele Youngblood:

I had a client that was moving to the Washington, D.C. area. Alex had sent out a lot of the emails of who he was and what areas he served. I really liked the way that the emails were presented. I looked up his website. It had a nice presentation. I called him. We talked on the phone, and then I was very comfortable with him, so I sent my client to him. She's still in the process of looking in the Washington, D.C. area, but I was comfortable because I already knew him, and knew that he would take great care of my client.

Alex Saenger:

Michele and I connected initially, through the Real Agent Advice videos. When we had a networking event at Keller Williams Family Reunion, and then another one at Mega Camp, we were actually able to meet in person, and have a conversation, in addition to speaking on the phone and everything else.

Michele became very comfortable with me through the interactions that we had. She felt so comfortable that she actually sent me a client referral. That is exactly the relationship I would like to have with you. Something where you and I can work together, to help one of my clients and to help one of your clients, regardless of where we are. We're helping each other and we're actually sending and exchanging referral fees.

The problem is you know who I am and the market I serve (Washington, D.C., MD and VA), but I don't know where you serve. So connect with me through the KW Referral or Kelle platforms if you are in KW. Be sure to mention this book (RAA). Or if you are outside of KW, send me an email at coffee@RealAgentAdvice.com. Let's get to know each other, and I can add you to my database to send you a referral when I have one to share!

The Agent on the Other Side

JoAnn Callaway, Scottsdale, Arizona

THE AGENT
ON THE OTHER SIDE

JoAnn Callaway:

Take care of the agent on the other side. They are wonderful, wonderful people. If you just take two minutes to get to know them. If they aren't having a good day, maybe you could bring a little sunshine into it. But I think the very most important thing is just to let them know you're there. If you have two good agents, one on each side, you can make any deal in town work.

Alex Saenger:

Isn't it interesting? Someone that's been in the business for 20 years talks about one of the most important things about a transaction is actually treating the other agent, on the other side, with respect and dignity. Treating them like an agent that you want to work with. And what's interesting about that is, I have found there really are two types of agents. There are collaborative agents and there are confrontational agents. The confrontational agents never win, the collaborative ones, they do win. So keep in mind, in any transaction it takes two good agents to make it a success.

Why Going to Big Events is Great for Networking and Referrals

Tom Harmon, Frisco, Colorado

WHY GOING TO BIG EVENTS IS GREAT FOR NETWORKING AND REFERRALS

Tom Harmon:

You should come to events like Keller Williams Family Reunion, because you get to meet a lot of neat people.

Alex Saenger:

What happens here?

Tom Harmon:

We get to network with everybody throughout the United States, and in our market. It's a secondary home market. People send you referrals from all over the United States.

Alex Saenger:

When you think about networking, a lot of times agents focus on whom they know locally. But if you want the opportunity to network with agents from across the nation, get out of your state. Go travel. Go to a Keller Williams event. Go to a Buffini event. Go to a Mike Ferry event. Go to a Tony Robbins event. Go to something outside of your area. Why? Because the people that actually attend those events are typically the most successful agents in their market. Why? Because the agents that aren't very successful, well, quite frankly, they can't afford to go. Who better to network with than the agents that are actually going to some of these big events?

Utilizing Networking Groups

Kathy Baker, Appleton, Wisconsin

Kathy Baker:

Join a networking group of some kind. I became a member of our local builders association, and two years after I was in the business, I started working with a builder, and got to work with him for ten years until his wife got her license.

Alex Saenger:

Networking is one of those things that you can do in so many different ways. You can join a chamber of commerce. You can get involved in a group. Getting in front of other people and other businesses is one of the best ways to actually get referrals from those businesses.

One of the places you can go if you're looking to network and make new friends, and enjoy yourself at the same time, is Meetup. Go to Meetup.com, find a group of something that you're interested in, get involved, and just start networking with those people. You'll be amazed at what you can do while you're having fun. You can actually generate business by connecting with those people during those networking events.

How Business Referrals Bring in Clients

Jason Van Stiphout, Oshawa, Ontario, Canada

HOW BUSINESS REFERRALS BRING IN CLIENTS

Jason Van Stiphout:

I am business to business. I basically have a very tight network of people that I work with and with whom I can help any of my clients. I bring to the table a portfolio of people to help with anything. Anything that they need, I'm the guy they call and say, "Who do I call?" That's probably my unique thing. The business people that I'm working with for business to business, I'm always asking them, "How can I help your business?" But then I ask in return, "I need you to give me a referral name."

Alex Saenger:

Just last week, my daughter was over at one of her friend's houses, and the dad and I were talking. We were talking about his house and some of the things he might want to do to it like open up a wall and different things. He said, "You know what, Alex? Can you come out here and look at this?" He showed me his portico, and the portico should be flat, and it was kind of leaning down, and he was like, "Is that normal?" I'm like, "That's not normal."

When we talked a little bit more, he asked, "Do you have somebody that you can recommend that could fix it?" I said, "I've got exactly the right person." Those kinds of connections, and being that kind of resource for your community and the people that you're interacting with, are what real estate is all about. It's about connecting businesses together, and connecting businesses to your customers. By doing that, you're showing your value to not only your customer, but also to your business relationships. After all, if you think about somebody that is fixing a roof, do you think that person might know somebody that might be moving? They do! And they send you referrals. And you send them referrals. It's a wonderful thing.

If you don't have a great business network, you should put one together. Make sure you have professionals in every house-related category. If you're not getting referrals from your business network, make sure you do it. Make sure you build that network, and make sure you help your clients with the best professionals.

Why You Need to Tell Your Stories

Teresa Souvignier, Palo Alto, California

Teresa Souvignier:

I think an asset is just my ability to connect with people on a friendly level. Then I tell a few little stories about how one deal almost didn't go through but I saved it by doing X, Y, Z. And then, suddenly they think, wow she knows what's she's doing, or she has inside information about maybe off-market listings, that kind of thing. So it doesn't take much to impress people.

I learned when I was at Keller Williams training, tell your stories. So there was a time when there were four other offers for a property. One was a cash offer and I had a 10%-down buyer. I developed a relationship with the listing agent, showed up in person with my offer, and also brought cookies. So we got to be sort of buddies, and then, he wanted his clients to work with me. He had a feeling that my deal would go through and he wasn't sure about the all-cash offer. So he did the deal with me.

Alex Saenger:

Stories. Who doesn't love a good story? Recently, I did a Millionaire Real Estate Investors seminar, and in the seminar, one of the things that I focused on, was my personal experience as a real estate investor. After the class, one of the agents that was attending came up to me and said, "You know what Alex? The most powerful part of that presentation was when you got into your own personal stories. When you talked about the flip opportunities that you did. When you talked about the investment for buy and hold opportunities and showed the actual cash flow and showed the actual numbers and talked about the details, about how that happened and the timeframe." When I got into the story of actually what I was working on and what I dealt with, the audience connected with me on a much deeper level because they could understand and they could relate to me as the person doing all these things.

They too could see themselves being that person relating to and doing all these things. It's really important when you're dealing with your clients and when you're dealing with other real estate agents that if there's a story you have that ties into what you're talking about, go ahead and tell the story. Chances are they want to hear about it.

They want to hear how you handled it and what the outcome was. Your story is evidence of success. It's evidence of failure. It is evidence that you've been through it before and that you've learned and that you're going to give them the benefit of that lesson and wisdom.

Don't be Afraid to Ask for Advice From Other Agents

Jessica Carter, Ann Arbor, Michigan

Jessica Carter:

If you are a new agent, be open to support, and take more agents out to lunch. Ask a lot of questions. "How do you get a client? What's a deal look like? What happens when the inspection doesn't go right?" Those nuts and bolts parts of the deal. The things that come up when you're new and you're just like "What do I do?" That kind of thing.

Alex Saenger:

Before I became a real estate professional, and I was really focused on selling houses, I actually owned a virtual tour company. I did that for about six years. Every time I went in, I had a conversation with the agent. I asked "So, how'd you get this listing? Oh, really, you met them through soccer?" Or, "Oh, really, they were a neighbor of yours?" Or, "Oh really, they're in your farm area?" Whatever it was, I always asked, "So how'd you get this piece of business?" Because I wanted to find out what were the prevailing trends that were happening in the real estate business in terms of lead generation and acquiring a new client.

I wound up getting into real estate, and I've been doing the business for 15 years. Asking those questions is something that really allowed me to get some great information from other agents. Similarly, now as an agent, who is quite frankly thriving in the business, and able to reach out to people like you right now through this book, you're effectively asking me the question, "What do you think about this topic that we happen to be talking about here or in another interview?" It's a way for us to connect, and a way for me to give back to you so that you can learn.

Find agents in your local market, whose business methods you admire, and take them out to coffee, or to lunch, (or on a Caribbean cruise if you're thinking of me) and have a conversation. Find out what they're doing, and chances are, if they're at a great broker like I am, you're going to find that they're willing to share. They're willing to share and both of you can grow in your businesses.

I'm going to invite you to maybe have coffee with me. Next time you head out to one of the national events, like Keller Williams Family Reunion, or Mega Camp, or even a Mastermind, get in touch with me. Let's have coffee. Let's exchange ideas. Let's talk. In fact, I might even feature you on a Real Agent Advice video episode.

Learn From an Agent That is Doing Better Than You

Lisa Mutschler, Wheat Ridge, Colorado

Lisa Mutschler:

Hang out with people who are doing better than you, and who are at a place in their business where you want to be. People will share their ideas on what it took to get there, and that will make you strive to really be the best that you can be.

Alex Saenger:

One of the things that I found so incredible about Keller Williams is the fact that you have so many people willing to share what they are doing. They are willing to let you be inspired by what they have accomplished, by learning and watching what they've done with their businesses, and seeing how they did it. Think about that for a second, and think about where you are in your business. Find some people that you might be able to look at and say, "You know, I'd really love to learn from that person," and then spend some time with them. Take them out for coffee. Have lunch with them.

Ultimately, this book is exactly for that purpose, to give you that inspiration and insight from so many agents across the nation. After all, it is our company wide culture to share. Sharing with over 160,000 agents. Now that is a powerful movement. Are you a part of something that big? If you're not, get in touch with me now, and let's connect: coffee@RealAgentAdvice.com.

Seeking Out Talented and Successful Mentors

Andrea Beem, Albany, Oregon

SEEKING OUT TALENTED AND SUCCESSFUL MENTORS

Andrea Beem:

Find someone in your market center that is achieving in this industry at a high level, and latch on to them from the very beginning. More than likely they'll be willing to help you, and it will help you start out your business right. Most people don't start out their business without some sort of plan, or some sort of education, or learning, and this industry is such that unless you go and seek that out, you won't have that. So seek it out.

Alex Saenger:

Seeking out talent is one of the key things in being successful in real estate. It's not just about becoming a team member, or seeking out talent to join your team when you're a more successful agent, and you've done this for a while, and you're starting to build and grow your team. Seeking out talent is also something you do right in the very beginning. Finding that person that would be a great mentor for you is one of the best things you could possibly do. A mentor is going to help you skip a lot of the mistakes they made, and get right to the stuff that's gold. Right to the stuff that's going to make you the most productive agent you can be.

One of those things is making a plan. Do your 1-3-5 (a method of goal setting). If you haven't done one yet, get it done now. Don't forget about learning. Take advantage of all the classes and all the education that Keller Williams has to offer. There's so much available to you every day of the week. In fact, the Real Agent Advice videos and chapters are some of those pieces. Not just Real Agent Advice, but the KW system, and the KWConnect educational platform. Tremendous amounts of content and tremendous amounts of video content are available from other agents. There are video materials, written materials, and there are classes. If you haven't tapped into that stuff, check it out, it's awesome.

Role Models

Sujatha Bhaskara, Morganville, New Jersey

Sujatha Bhaskara:

Surround yourself with people who could be role models, people that have already done it. Go on the path that's proven to get to the level of success that you want and deserve.

I think meeting some of those key people I'm going to stay connected with is important. They're going to help me grow not only in my business, but as a person. I've met some people that are looking to grow, and I've met some people that are further along the line of where I need to be. So it's been growth in all different aspects. I think that's fantastic.

Alex Saenger:

Recently, we had our Washington, D.C. metro area Regional Mastermind. What's amazing about the panel we had, is that everyone on the panel, in fact everyone on several panels, was focused specifically on growth. Chris Suarez is heading up the growth initiative for Keller Williams for expansion teams and is showing people why expansion is actually so important. If you want to talk about growth, these are some heavy hitters.

Sarah Reynolds is in our local market. I remember knowing her when she did a couple dozen transactions a year. Now her team is up to 411 closed transactions in a year. These are the kinds of people that I want to surround myself with, so that I can grow and learn from them and see where I can take my own business.

Wendy Papasan, the wife of Jay Papasan, had grown her business. Not just her business, but her financial situation as a family.

Surrounding yourself with powerful people that have gone before you, people who have proven how the systems and models available at Keller Williams can lead to success, and have become so successful by surrounding themselves with other equally impressive people, is one of the ways that you can accelerate your business.

The Power of Associating Yourself With the Right People

Rich Ganim, Sarasota, Florida

THE POWER OF ASSOCIATING YOURSELF WITH THE RIGHT PEOPLE

Rich Ganim:

Surrounding myself with people that do more, know more, and have more than I have is important. One of the biggest things that I learned in my career is that if you want to be broke, hangout with broke people. If you want to be successful, hangout with successful people.

What I learned very quickly is that the habits of the broke continue, and the habits of the successful continue. And you chose whether you want to be broke or you want to be successful, to whatever degree. You have to make a decision one way or the other in your personal life about where you want to live so that in your professional life it comes through.

Alex Saenger:

Think about the people that you spend the most time with in your circle of friends and at work. Also, think about how much money you make, what your personality is like, what you wear, and all those types of things. You are an average of the people that you spend the most time with. Now, it may sound callous, but if you want to upgrade your situation, upgrade the company you keep. Affiliating themselves with people that they look up to is one of the things that allows people to grow in their wealth and grow personally.

Real Estate is About Relationships

Mariana Costa, Centerville, Massachusetts

Mariana Costa:

"Relationships," is the name of the game. Relationships can help you leverage your business for the rest of your life. Remember to focus on your relationships, because they're going to be the relationships that are going to feed your business for the rest of your career, and will help you take your business to the next level whenever you're ready for it.

Alex Saenger:

When you think about relationships, each individual person that you build a relationship with can actually extend how many people you're connected with. For example, one person that I might have a connection with actually might introduce me to two other people. Those two other people, in turn, might introduce me to three other people who then in turn might introduce me to three more people. Just having a relationship with this first person can actually introduce me to a whole network and a whole path of other relationships.

This is one of the reasons why, when you first get started in the real estate business, things start off slowly. Over time, business slowly builds. Each one of these relationships can turn into a different source of referrals. When you're thinking about relationships, think about the idea that every relationship that you establish at a genuine level (being who you are) is going to generate a plethora of opportunity.

Breeding Success

Cole Whisenhunt, Lubbock, Texas

Cole Whisenhunt:

I think real estate comes back to relationships. Whether that's somebody you've known for a long time, or someone you meet at an initial buyer's consultation. Whatever it is, how you develop that relationship, and how that trust is being built, is going to breed success.

I think a lot of my success has come through people who knew, before I was in real estate, in sales, that they could trust me. So when I got into real estate, I wasn't selling them. I was being a friend, and I was looking out for them. I was the natural choice for them.

Alex Saenger:

What's interesting about real estate is you can come to another person from two different places. You can come to them from the direction of real estate, or you can come to them from the place of trust.

Either one is a great starting point. Think about before you got into real estate, you had lots of people that you knew that trusted you as an individual. As a person. Right? So the trust piece was already built. Now it was just a matter of shifting them from just trusting you in the way they knew you, into trusting you in relation to real estate.

That's the bridge that you have to cross when you are getting started in real estate: where you've built a relationship with somebody, and real estate hasn't come up yet.

The second way is the reverse. First, you start with real estate, and then you have to build trust with potential customers so that they want to work with you and actually do a transaction with you.

Now, there are a lot of systems and tools we can put in place. If you start from a place of real estate, and then bring them to trust, you can go through a questionnaire, a buyer consultation, a listing presentation, and things like that. You're building trust. You're mirroring and matching, and building rapport along the way. Those are all things that are going to wind up building trust.

You give them advice. They make a mistake. They realize the advice you gave them was good advice, and now they trust you more. So you can build that trust over time. But it takes time.

The other way is to start with the trust already established. "I trust you as a person that's honest, that's going to be fair with me." And now it's a matter of showing them that you have expertise in real estate. That can be done through social media. It can be done through sending them success stories that you've had with other clients. It can be done through testimonials. You might show them properties you've sold.

Which direction you're coming from impacts the strategy that you're going to use. Most of the time, which strategy you're going to use is going to depend on how long you've been in the business.

New people are going to have people with trust, and they need to build the relationship for real estate. People that have been in the business for a lot longer are going to have the real estate side. They're going to get referred to other people, and they're going to have to build the trust.

Reasons to be Real on Social Media

Arnita Greene, Upper Marlboro, Maryland

Arnita Greene:

Social media has been another part of my success. I post a lot. Not just real estate, but my life. What goes on day to day interacting with my clients. Whether it's a closing or when it's a walk through, when I'm just walking through with the client to show a house.

Don't just post about the good things of real estate, you want to also let them know the lows of it too. Everything isn't always good. Let the people into your life and let people know what's going on and know that it's not always a happy thing in real estate. Sometimes it's a low. A lot of times it's a low.

Everybody is a potential client. They might not use you now, but sooner or later, they're going to call you. It happens all the time.

Alex Saenger:

Do you ever notice on social media how people are just like, "My life is perfect. Everything is awesome."? Everybody focuses on the positive. That's what she's talking about here. If you're going to make social media part of your plan, part of your strategy to connect with people, you want them to see who you genuinely are.

In real estate, if you're going to be posting, it's okay to post things that happen in your daily life as a real estate agent. In fact, in my opinion, some of the most popular YouTube channels when it comes to real estate, are agents talking about their daily struggles and daily things that they're dealing with in their real estate business.

So if you're going to go down that road, go ahead and post it. You know, "I'm at a settlement," or, "Hey I'm touring a home with a client." Or, "I'm at a broker's open." Or you know, "My sign just fell down. I have to go fix it because a big nor'easter came and threw it down on the ground."

It's real life and it's really about you. But it's also about real estate. It's not just, "Hey here's a new listing."

So if you're thinking about doing things with social media, take some of her tips and maybe focus on some of those aspects to add to your posts and enhance your social media.

Simple Tips for Engaging Millennials

Jenney Szeto, Cambridge, Massachusetts

Jenney Szeto:

Right now I'm generating a lot of leads through Facebook groups. I'm running webinars and mostly, for me, it's just messaging through different Facebook portals that I'm involved in. I'm involved with a group that's all about millennials, people such as social impact change makers. They are the kind of people interested in developing as leaders, and for me, I was offering advice about buying a home. So many of them have worked for many years and they've been renting their whole lives and they're ready to make that shift. They don't know how they can start buying real estate because they've only ever been renting. That's kind of how I've been networking through Facebook, to be able to offer them that advice.

Alex Saenger:

I love the approach that Jenney's taking for her lead generation sources. She's leveraging the group that she's affiliated with, the millennial group. She's leveraging people that want to have social impact. She's focusing on Facebook. She's focusing on people that have been renting forever and now they're getting ready to transition into buyers. They're taking the next step in their financial future by investing in their home that they're going to actually live in and make money off of. Finding a niche in your business is a really great way to get connected with your client base and, in this case, if you're focused on millennials, you might want to do some of the things that Jenney's doing as well.

Chapter Four:

Database

Introduction

In real estate, your database of people is important. The bigger your database, the more business you have. It's just that simple. And it's important to start it early. In this chapter, you'll learn about databases.

You'll also learn about the basic information you can have in your database, and you'll read about organizing and subcategorizing your database and the different options you have for maintaining one.

You'll read the lesson about why you should add people to your database consistently and systematically. You'll also get ideas for adding people, such as starting with your sphere of influence, asking for contact information, and a tip from Alex for having people put their contact information into your phone.

Additionally, you'll get advice about communicating with your database regularly and consistently. You'll learn about the importance of this and how, when you communicate with people in your database you should provide value for them.

Your database is a very important source of leads, referrals and business. It is something you should start early and organize, and something you should add to and communicate with regularly.

This chapter should inspire you to start a database if you don't have one. And if you do have a database already, it should give you ideas for making yours better.

Database Basics: Name, Address And ...???

Leo Robles, Corona, California

DATABASE BASICS: NAME, ADDRESS AND...???

Leo Robles:

So number one, the first thing that I would do, is I would start to develop my database from day one. I didn't do that. I wish somebody would have told me, "Hey, you know what? Plug in your database." Get just name, number, email, and address, just as simple as that, and then put it on a systematic database so that you can actually drip to these clients, so you can build your business that way.

Alex Saenger:

We always talk about databases, but we don't necessary talk about what makes a database. The good news is that it doesn't have to be a professionally developed computer database tool. It could be a software program spreadsheet. It could be a piece of paper where you write things down. Or it could be note cards that you keep. In fact, Gary Keller started his business just with note cards. The bottom line is, you just really need five basic pieces of information to build your database.

Number one, name. Make sure you have people spell their first and last names. How do you spell John? Or is it Jon? That's right, there are different ways to spell it. Two, you want to make sure that you get their address. Which address? Their email address or their mailing address? Well, you want both, so that's three pieces of information. Next, you want to make sure you have their cellphone number. Why their cellphone, not their home phone nor their business phone? Because you can't text those other numbers. Make sure you have their cellphone number.

Then finally, I like to get their birthday. We don't need the year, just the month and the day, because I like to celebrate birthdays. After all, from whom do you get a birthday card? Maybe your mom, maybe your spouse, and maybe one of your kids. What I like to do is stick a scratch off lottery ticket in there. It's just a neat little gift. I had a client that just thanked me the other day for that who won $2.

So, when you build your database, make sure you get those five critical pieces of information, and then you can start marketing to the people in your database.

Learn to Manage Your Database With a System That Works For You

Carol Simenson, Bismarck, North Dakota

Carol Simenson:

If I would have asked, "How do you manage your contact database?" Back then, in the '80s or '90s, they would have said, "What are you talking about?"

Alex Saenger:

But today?

Carol Simenson:

But today, you know, what do you do with your contacts, how do you mange that?

Alex Saenger:

So what is a database? A database is a list of names, contacts, email addresses, mailing addresses, and dates of birth, of relationships that you have. And how you organize that information really is completely up to you.

Some people use something as simple as their cellphone to maintain their database. They take notes in there. They put associations in there.

In fact, we have one agent in our office who's actually one of our top producers. He's sold over 40 transactions this year and did about $20 million in business, and he manages his entire database right from his phone.

Another way people do it, is they'll use Microsoft Excel and just create a spreadsheet. They'll keep notes about the people and the conversations they have. You could get more sophisticated. You could use a system like eEdge, Top Producer, Referral Maker, or the new KWCommand. These are more sophisticated tools that are specifically designed for real estate.

Other people might use a contact management service like MailChimp, or

Constant Contact, or BombBomb.

What system you use, really doesn't matter. What matters, is that you put the information in the database, you record the conversations and the relationships you have with people, and you make sure that you stay in constant contact with those people.

Having the information all in one place is important. Not a few business cards in your desk drawer, some people in your phone, some people in your email, and some people on your social media. They all need to be in one place so that you can manage those relationships.

Know How to Manage Your Database

Karen Judd, Arlington, Texas

Karen Judd:

What I would have really liked to have known about, is how to get into the database. How to manage that database, and really how to work the database. It took me a while to get up and running. I went to different classes in our market center, but I didn't really feel like I got to where I needed to be with everything, because I had to put pieces together.

Alex Saenger:

Karen is talking about using a database. Of course, there is a technical side to this. This will depend on the specific database you use. One thing though, that is fundamental to all databases, and to starting your business, is organizing your database. This is a critical component of using your database well.

I'm a certified instructor for the Peak Producers system from Brian Buffini. He gets into how to organize your actual database. Keller Williams also has a similar model that helps you define who you should be focusing on and how to actually approach that. Focusing on your database is the fastest way to get started. It's the thing that you should do first.

Why You Should Subcategorize Your Database

Kathy Baker, Appleton, Wisconsin

Kathy Baker:

Start a database right away of everybody you meet, no matter how insignificant the meeting. Sort the people by how you know them so that you have a really good understanding of how you can help them in the future. I've been doing that for 22 years, and I have a huge database.

Alex Saenger:

So when Kathy talks about your database, she mentions to make sure you put everyone you meet in your database. You're going to have lots of different categories. A lot of times agents put people in their database, but they only have one category, the database. You need to make sure that you subcategorize people.

For example, you're going to have people in your sphere, the people that you're friends with, the people that you send your holiday cards to. You're also going to have people within your farm areas, people that live in your neighborhood or farm area that you're marketing to. You might have nationwide referral agents, (people like me hint, hint), in your database or other agents in your local market that you want to market to in terms of listings that you have coming on the market or a need that you have for a buyer. You might also have contractors or even lenders, or in my case, I actually have a tiny little subgroup of people that I know that like to play cards (there's actually a full house of them wink, wink). So that's a different way to organize your database. Having people categorized in specific areas, specific niches, allows you to tailor your message to a focused group instead of using a broad brushstroke.

Use Your Sphere of Influence

Chris Upham, Northern Virginia

Chris Upham:

Start with a database of your sphere of influence, people who know you, like you, and trust you. Aim for 200 people … you should have that. What type of database you have, is irrelevant. If you have a spreadsheet that's got first name, last name, email, phone number, street address, city, state, and zip code, and you have that complete information for 200 people, you have a database. Then you're able to be in touch with those people with meaningful contacts 36 times in a year, which interestingly enough is in alignment with The Millionaire Real Estate Agent Lead Generation Model. That is the lowest cost, highest return on investment, highest conversion rate way of developing business there is.

Alex Saenger:

Chris is talking about The Millionaire Real Estate Agent book, and he's talking about the Lead Generation Model. There's a great segment in the book that talks specifically about lead generation and how your database is the cornerstone to your business. He talks about 200 names. If you get a bit more, and have 240 names of people you can call, you're going to generate 40 transactions that year just from your database. That assumes you are consistently marketing to them each 36 times over a 12 month period. The numbers hold true across the board and regardless of market. I know the ratios apply to my business, and they will apply to yours as well.

Connect With New People to Expand Your Database

Gloria Frazier, Montgomery, Alabama

Gloria Frazier:

Your database is key. That's your net worth. Work your database. You have to connect with people, you have to meet people, and you have to manage that database.

Alex Saenger:

Your database is the fundamental core component of your business. The bigger the database, the more business you're going to do. You have to nurture that database, and you have to feed the database. One of my favorite ways to feed the database is actually with the Keller Williams mobile app. It's a great way to talk to people, and say, "Hey, are you looking for homes? Here, let me share my mobile app with you. You can search for homes nearby using the GPS on your phone."

The point of that is to make sure, number one, they have your app on their phone, but number two, and probably even more important, that you're getting their personal information so that you can stay in touch with them and build your database.

Do you Know the Easiest Way to Get Someone's Information?

Erin Chappelle, Westlake, Ohio

Erin Chappelle:

I would be a lot more systematic with my database. I'm still not great at it. I know what I need to do, but I'm not doing it at 100%. I would have started really doing that correctly, getting everybody in there, getting them on a plan, and feeding it consistently. I have random eight by eights, or thirty three touches, or different follow ups. Sometimes I put people on and sometimes I don't. I don't have a great system for being consistent with who is in my database, so not everybody's in my database. That's still a work in progress.

Alex Saenger:

So would you say consistency is important?

Erin Chappelle:

Oh, huge. Huge.

Alex Saenger:

One of the things that I do when I meet somebody is I'll pull out my phone, and I'll ask them to go ahead and fill out some contact information. The reason for that is because, if I hand you my phone, and it has a blank contact in it, chances are you're going to type in the correct spelling of your first name and last name. You're going to enter your cell phone number. You might even enter your email address. Some people even go so far as to enter their mailing address.

What's amazing about handing somebody your phone with a blank contact is, you get way more information, way more accurately than if you were to just hand them a business card. How does that relate to your database? Because this is one of the sources you can use to consistently add names to your database. It's a phenomenal tool that I learned and I'm sharing it with you, so that you can do the same thing, and it's super easy.

So, if you want to add more people to your database in a consistent way, hand them your phone with a blank contact, and you'll be surprised at how many contacts you can get in just one day.

Start Your Day With Your Database

Cheryl Coleman, Huntington Beach, California

Cheryl Coleman:

I actually spent an hour talking to Tony DiCello, and that turned my whole business around. That one hour changed everything.

Alex Saenger:

What did that conversation entail?

Cheryl Coleman:

9 a.m. to noon every day you work on your database. You don't do anything else. We even had our meetings in the morning, and he said, "Don't go to them."

We ended up changing our market center meetings because of Tony DiCello. But it changed everything. My database is huge now. I don't work it enough, that's still a goal, but we're the top team. We've been so for two years. We're doing fantastic. We're going to close six million by the end of this month for this year already.

Alex Saenger:

One of the key factors in any business, not just in real estate, is your database. And your database you'll see, in Gary Keller's The Millionaire Real Estate Agent on page 143, is the center of your business generation engine. Now when you listen to Gary Keller, he says, "If you want to double your business, double your database, because that's the source of all of your business."

How to Develop the "Every Day" Database Mindset

Mary Anne Walser, Atlanta, Georgia

Mary Anne Walser:

Call your database every day. It's not really anything all of us don't know, right? You just call people and talk to them. Think about contribution. Come from contribution, and that makes all the difference.

Alex Saenger:

Your number one thing in your 1-3-5, in your 3 section, is your database, your sphere. Focusing on your sphere for your lead generation is probably the most critical component to generating business. Your database is your rock. It's where you're going to get most of your business every year.

What Mary Anne also talked about was coming from contribution. When you communicate with your database, you want to make sure that you're coming to them with contribution. It's much better to give, and then ask. In other words, let me give you an item of value. Let me give you a pie at Thanksgiving, and then let me ask, "By the way, whom do you know that might be thinking about buying or selling in the next year? I'd love to help them." It's much easier to make that request and ask when you're coming from a contribution.

Remember That You Are Providing Value

Cole Whisenhunt, Lubbock, Texas

REMEMBER THAT YOU ARE PROVIDING VALUE

Cole Whisenhunt:

The first tactic or strategy I wish I would have implemented sooner would have been really feeding my database.

We hear that it's a data bank, instead of your database, because those are the people that already love you, trust you, and may want to help you. And so I reached out to everybody. I took a step back though because I didn't want to be too much of a "salesperson" and I felt that I was being that way.

I realized though I really am providing value. Somebody's either going to call a sign, they're going to get an online lead, they're going to call an office, and if I'm friends with them and they know they can trust me, they know I'm going to give great service. I thought I might as well be the one that's informing them on the market, to help educate them so they feel comfortable and confident.

Feeding into my database, and spending my dollars there earlier on, would be the main thing that I would've changed.

Alex Saenger:

Cole talks about your data bank. You may have heard that before. Why do we think of our database as our data bank? Who's in our database? People we care about. People that, if they're thinking about doing anything with real estate, we want to make sure they get the right advice to make the best decision.

After all, when you call them, you owe it to them and to yourself. Why? Because you want to make sure they're getting the best advice. You don't want them going to some other agent, who maybe doesn't know as much about their situation, or about what they're interested in, as you might.

You have an obligation to reach out to those people and give them the information they need to make the best decisions. You need to stay in touch with them.

Why Having a Far Reaching Database is Essential to Your Business

Lee Potts, Kahului, Maui, Hawaii

Lee Potts:

Really focusing on our database, and taking care of those people and understanding how internet marketing works, is important, because 80-90% of our clients don't live in our area. We're on an island in the Pacific, 2,500 miles from the mainland, and the majority of our clients live on the mainland or in Canada or in another country.

Alex Saenger:

So my question for you is, how broad is your database? If you take the Potts' case, their database isn't a lot of local people, it's a lot of international or domestic people outside of the islands of Hawaii. Ultimately, you can source your business from a lot of different places. It's not just local.

You might get client referrals from people that no longer live in your area. So keeping them on your database is really important. You can also get investors, not just locally, but internationally. Not to mention other agents referring new business from across the country. So your database isn't just one group of people, it's a whole set of different types of people that are going to affect your business in different ways. Making sure that you have a plan to communicate with those different types of people is really important.

One of my core groups is my sphere and another one is my referral network. That includes agents like you. I want you in my network so we can exchange referrals. I'm never too busy for your referrals, are you too busy for mine? Let's connect!

Double Your Database and You'll Double Your Business

Erin Chappelle, Westlake, Ohio

Erin Chappelle:

Putting people in your database is important. They could be people that you meet, current clients, past clients, or potential clients. It's important to be adding systematically, whether it be two to five contacts a day, to have a system for that, and to have a plan. I don't, so I randomly may add people at certain times. My database is not up-to-date. I would definitely stick with updating your database in a systematic way. Have a goal for every day such as, what you're going to do with that database, how many people you're going to add, whether you're going to follow up, and how that's going to look.

Alex Saenger:

So, as you know, if you want to double your business, double your what? Your database. And what's the easiest way to double your database? Well, think about it this way. Let's say you had a database of 500 people and you wanted to double that. There are 52 weeks in the year and you're going to take a couple of them off, so let's just use 50 weeks that you're going to actually add people to your database. 500 people, that's 10 people a week or two people a workday. Now, that's something I think you can do. Well, if you do that, you're going to find that you actually are on track to doubling your business next year just simply by adding two people to your database every day. Is it something you can do? I know it's something I can do, so let's both do it, and let's do it today.

Your Database is Your Data Bank

Jackie Ellis, Boynton Beach, Florida

Jackie Ellis:

When I first got started, I wish somebody had told me to start building a database and taught me how to systematically communicate with it, and to always provide value to that database. I don't feel like I heard the word database. In fact, on my real estate team, we now call it a data bank because we think that's where the money is.

Alex Saenger:

If you think about a database, or a data bank as Jackie calls it, it is your source of revenue. In fact, in Gary Keller's The Millionaire Real Estate Agent book, he talks about the fact that for every 12 people you have in your database, you should be able to do two transactions a year.

Now, that might be directly or indirectly through a referral. Ultimately, if you have, let's say 240 people in your phone, people that you know, that actually know you, you should be able to do 20 transactions, just from the people in your phone, if you did half the rate that was mentioned.

So make sure you get your database organized. Make sure you get all the information in there: name, phone number, email address, mailing address, even birthday. Stay in touch with those people and you should be able to turn your database into a data bank.

Your Database: The One Thing That No Other Agent Will Have

Dianna Kokoszka, Austin, Texas

YOUR DATABASE: THE ONE THING THAT NO OTHER AGENT WILL HAVE

Dianna Kokoszka:

For agents just starting out in the business, you should absolutely build your database every single day, because this is the one thing that no other agent is going to have. It's something that will set you apart. When you look in your phone, I'll bet you ten to one you have about 2,500 to 3,000 people in your phone if you really look. Start calling them.

Alex Saenger:

One of the things Dianna mentions in there, is that your database is unique to you. And here's a little tip that I wanted to share with you. She talks about pulling out your phone, and pulling up all those contacts in your phone, and starting to make phone calls. After you make those phone calls to the people, one of the great things you can talk to them about is, "Do you have my mobile app? Do you have a way to search for homes right from your phone using the GPS?"

One of the things I did is, I actually put together a text message. I sent it out to all of them, and here it is. I'm going to share this with you. It's a great tip. You can do this yourself. It's an easy way to stay connected and to connect with them.

"Passing a home with a for sale sign? Curious about the price, photos and more? Download my free GPS enabled app." Enter the link. "You don't have to buy a house to be curious." Use a happy emoji, such as winking or a smiley face. "Works anywhere in the United States and Canada."

I can tell you right now, I have people contacting me constantly when I send this out, saying, "You know what, that's a great idea. I'll go ahead and do that." Because those that live on the phone, are the ones that win. And your database, is the place to start. And that database is unique to you.

Chapter Five:

Lead Generation

Introduction

Hold on. Stop. Put down this book. Go lead generate. No really, go lead generate. It's important. It's very important. Go do it - Now!

Welcome back … One of the main ideas you should take away from this book is that of generating leads, or as we call it, lead generation. Also known as "Lead Gen," lead generation is extremely important for your business. If you don't generate leads, you won't have a business.

As you try to generate leads, you probably want to know about some things. If you are just starting out, you might wonder, from whom you can generate leads. Wherever you are in your business, you might be curious about different lead generation tactics. You might also wonder how often you should lead generate, and how you interact with people to generate leads.

All of these things are addressed in this chapter. Through the interviews, you'll gain a wealth of information to help you in your lead generation efforts.

If you're wondering whom to generate leads from, if you are just starting out, you'll gain some insight. You'll learn about generating leads from your sphere of influence, people like your friends, family, and neighbors.

If you're curious about lead generation tactics, you've come to the right place. Whether you are just starting out, and you're looking for how to begin, or you have been in the business for a while, and are looking for new ideas, this chapter is a great resource.

You'll learn about putting on internal events and giveaways. You'll also learn about attending external events, such as bridal shows, and how they can be a source of leads.

If you're an online person, you too will find information. You'll learn about generating leads online and using social media and email to prospect for leads.

One great idea for generating leads that you'll learn about is listings. You'll learn about a number of lead generation opportunities that come from listings such as open houses, yard sticks/signs, directional signs, and door knocking opportunities.

Although it may seem like you are just socializing, this chapter will also inspire you to lead generate through coffees and lunches.

In addition to all this, you'll learn about generating leads through farming, phone calls, snail mail, and utilizing your database (there's a chapter about databases in the book as you know).

As you read about different lead generation ideas, you'll learn about the importance of changing your methods with the situation and learning new tactics from others. You'll also learn the very important lesson of not to buy leads. DON'T BUY LEADS!

As you think about all of these great lead generation methods, you may wonder how often you should lead generate. This chapter will give you a direct answer: every business day. Not only that, but you'll find out about the importance of time blocking hours each day for lead generation and the importance of generating leads regularly and consistently.

Now, with all these ideas for generating leads and the knowledge that you should do so for hours every day, you might be wondering how you actually go about it. This chapter will give you a place to start.

You'll find out that it's all right to talk to people about real estate (they actually want you to, and it's not that hard). You'll also learn about the importance of providing value and being a resource for people. Additionally, you'll discover the idea of scripts and systems for lead generation, and, you'll learn about analyzing the effectiveness of your lead generation methods.

It can't be said enough: lead generation is important. It might be the most important thing you do at work each day. It is central to the success of your business.

If you followed the advice above, you already did some lead generation before you read this. As another piece of advice, once you finish this chapter, you should go do lead generation again. It's that important.

Learn, be inspired, and go do your lead gen!

What is Lead Generation?

Willy Nelson (not the singer), Lee's Summit, Missouri

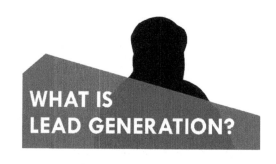

WHAT IS LEAD GENERATION?

Willy Nelson:

Lead generation. I have good lead generation. So when they tell you to do lead generation, you should do lead generation.

Alex Saenger:

What does that mean? What is lead generation?

Willy Nelson:

That's picking up the phone and calling people, whether it's your sphere of influence or its cold calling leads, or doing circle prospecting around your listings, if you have brand new listings … those kinds of things.

Alex Saenger:

So lead generation as defined in The Millionaire Real Estate Agent book is really broken up into three categories. First, you have to prospect and you have to engage in marketing. Second, you have to have a database and continually add people to it. Third, you have to market to the people in your database in an organized way. What's really interesting, is most people forget that the very first part about it is you have to prospect and you have to engage in marketing.

Myself, when I first got started in the real estate business, I focused more on the marketing and less on the prospecting. When you actually get into real estate you realize that the most successful agents are the ones that start first with a prospecting focus of lead generation and enhance it with the marketing aspect of things. So, for example, you'll call somebody that you know and you just ask, "Hey, by the way, if you knew somebody that was thinking about buying or selling real estate, do you have an agent that you'd refer them to?" "No I don't." "Could I be that person?" "Sure." Great, add their information to the database. That's called feeding the database.

Then you're going to systematically market to those people and make sure that you actually get in touch with them. Remind them that you're in real estate. That's the whole lead generation model. Focusing on that piece of your business is the number one most fundamental piece that you can focus on to build business, to build a profit, and to make your business successful.

Every Real Estate Professional Has Two Jobs ... Do You Know What They Are?

Lisa Mutschler, Wheat Ridge, Colorado

Lisa Mutschler:

Leads, and lead generating. I was not with Keller Williams when I first started. So that was huge. That was very huge.

Alex Saenger:

That's right, leads. Leads, leads, leads. As Gary Keller talks about in The Millionaire Real Estate Agent book on page 41 - "everyone has two jobs—their chosen profession and lead generation."[8] What does he mean? He says on pages 40 and 41, "To succeed in real estate, you must have client leads. It's that simple. Until you have enough leads (to meet or exceed your goals), there is no other issue. No matter if you are a doctor, lawyer, or entrepreneur, everyone has two jobs—their chosen profession and lead generation."[9]

Until you have enough leads to satisfy your specific goals, and your team's goals, nothing else matters. So focus on leads. What are you doing to generate leads? What's your strategy? What are your tactics? What's your 1-3-5? What's your 411? These are all terms in the KW training system. If you don't have a strategy for leads, you don't really have a business. So focus on leads and get your business going.

[8,9] The Millionaire Real Estate Agent by Gary Keller with Dave Jenks and Jay Papasan. Copyright © 2004 by McGraw-Hill Education

Don't Wait for the Phone to Ring

Michael Acquisto, San Antonio, Texas

DON'T WAIT FOR
THE PHONE TO RING

Michael Acquisto:

I got my license, went to an office, and they basically just said, "Wait for the phone to ring." I didn't work for Keller Williams at the time. We went out and met with builders, and talked with builders about their clients, and they added us on, but it wasn't us going out and banging the phone, learning how to talk to people on a one-to-one basis, and bringing them in.

Alex Saenger:

What Michael's really talking about is the old adage, "Give a man a fish, and he'll eat for a day. Teach a man to fish, and he'll eat for a lifetime." That is our philosophy at Keller Williams. We go through the effort of teaching you how to prospect so that you can generate your own leads. Whether it be Productivity Coaching, one-on-one coaching, or mentorship, we have the right tools and the right systems in place to teach you what you need to learn so that you can do your own lead generation and not depend on some other source.

Work Your Sphere to Get Your Business Off the Ground

Ada Wang, Houston, Texas

Ada Wang:

So, you know friends, right? So, you know your neighborhood? So you can start doing the business from your friends and neighborhood. And when you start, and get a first customer, after you serve them well, and professionally, they're going to refer business. That's why I always get my business from referrals.

Alex Saenger:

What Ada's talking about is, when you first get started in real estate, start with the people that you know. Start with your friends, family, and neighbors. Those are the people that are going to know you and trust you for who you are, and they're going to understand that you're building the skill set when it comes to real estate. Serve those people really well and ask for referrals. That is how you exponentially grow your business year after year. So start with your friends, start with your family, start with your neighbors, and build your business and build your database.

What Works for Some Might Not Work for Others

Michele Youngblood, Chesterfield, Michigan

WHAT WORKS FOR SOME MIGHT NOT WORK FOR OTHERS

Michele:

Sphere of influence, obviously. Also, new people being added. For example, Realtor.com, we do get some leads from them. We actually also just signed up with Homes.com as well. And then, we've done other events, like my other buyer's agent and I just started doing bridal shows.

I sort of figured, these people are getting married. They're probably thinking about buying a house at some point in the future, if not soon. And we were the only real estate agents there, so it worked out really well for us. And the vendors ended up being a very good lead source as well, so talk to vendors for sure.

Alex Saenger:

Michele talked about online leads and she talked about bridal shows. By the way, I've done both of those things, and they worked out miserably for me. But they worked out great for her. And the reason I bring that up is because just because something didn't work for me, doesn't mean it can't work for somebody else. And just because it didn't work for somebody else doesn't mean it can't work for me. Every business is unique, and every business is designed for the person running that business.

Take the bridal show experience. I did a bridal show. I thought "This is great. These people are getting married and they're going to need a place to live." Guess what, in my area in Washington, D.C., most of those people already had a place. They were moving in with the other person, or their parents were giving them a place. Whereas in Michigan, maybe that's not the case. So that really worked for somebody like Michele.

When you analyze what your strategies are for how you're going to do your lead generation, check them regularly and analyze the results. Analyze the work you're doing and the money you're spending. You might have to make an adjustment.

167

You might have to adjust how you're doing it, you might have to add some stuff or reduce some stuff, or you might decide, "I've been doing this for three months or six months or nine months, and I haven't really received the return that I was expecting." Maybe it's time to listen to that and say, "I need to change direction here. I need to stop doing that and do something else instead."

Making sure that you focus on how you do your business, making sure that it's a right fit for you, is super important. I know that I've made plenty of mistakes in my business, and I've had to make adjustments along the way. And you know what? My business is more exciting today than it ever has been. We're on track to a record year, and why? Because we've made adjustments along the way, and we've now gotten to a point where our systems and our models and our tactics and our lead generation are all headed in the right direction.

Using KW's Proven Systems to Generate Leads Effectively

Pam Jenkins, Danville, California

Pam Jenkins:

If I was just starting in real estate, I wish someone would tell me about lead generation, and how important it would be to be with a company that can support you with lead generation.

Alex Saenger:

Think about lead generation. It can be defined in so many different ways. One of the first things to understand is there are scripts for lead generation. You also need to understand there are systems for lead generation. Further, you need to understand that there is more than one way of doing it. Finding a system that works for you starts by looking at what other people before you have done. Keller Williams gives you the opportunity to go into their backend, KWConnect, and learn from tons of agents that have done it before you. They have different systems and different models that you can use. Make sure that you're in front of your clients with a proven, consistent system that's going to allow you to generate leads.

Intentional About Being Friendly

Teresa Souvignier, Palo Alto, California

Teresa Souvignier:

Cultivating new leads for your database is important. I'm finding, the more I think about contacting anyone in the community, for example, by going to the grocery store, or talking to the guy that comes to fix my computer, that it's amazing. You slip in a little information about, "I'm a real estate agent, so I really need this to work." Then, by the end of it, he's like, "Well, I think I might want to buy a house."

Everybody wants to talk about real estate. You meet people on planes and at weddings. It's when you're intentional about trying to be friendly with people, and then bring your profession into the conversation, you can get leads that way.

Alex Saenger:

You know the random strangers that you run into? You could run into them anywhere. You could run into them at the car wash, at the library, at the grocery store or at a kid's sports event. What you're trying to do when you meet those people, that you've never met before, is you're trying to find something in common. For example, maybe they're buying the same type of bread that you like and you're wondering why they enjoy it so much like you do, because you have this great recipe that you use it with.

Being friendly is such a key component to building those relationships, those impromptu relationships. Then, once you get to know them a little bit, what's great is you ask them, "By the way, what do you do for a living?" What you'll find is, that when they start talking about it, there's that awkward moment of silence where you're not talking and they're not talking and they're naturally going to ask you the question, "Well, what do you do?" And you're going to go, "Oh, I'm in real estate. I sell houses for a living." "Oh, really? How's the market?" "Well, it depends. Are you buying, selling, renting, or investing?" That's the answer that you should be giving.

Now all of a sudden the conversation has changed from just being nice and friendly and cordial and having a conversation about something you have in common, to now you're talking about real estate. Now you can go ahead and build on that process of getting their information, getting them added to your database, and all that kind of stuff. So, you can transition just about any friendly conversation into a conversation about real estate, also known as lead generation.

Reasons Not to Buy Leads

Eric Hudson, Las Vegas, Nevada

Eric Hudson:

Another thing is prospecting above trying to buy leads. All of these lead providers, they keep coming to you and saying the same thing over and over again. They're going to get you leads, but how great are they? It's easier to generate your own leads.

Alex Saenger:

So what Eric is talking about is that real estate is a contact sport. It means that you need to make phone calls, you need to have coffee with people, and you have to have lunches. Whatever it is, you've got to actually talk to people. Meet with them, talk with them on the phone, and get in touch with them. If you don't contact them, you can't generate a lead. Now, a lead from a real estate website that consumers might use, that's not really a lead. That's really an inquiry. Inquiries are not leads.

A lead is a referral from someone that you know that says, "I know somebody that's thinking about buying or selling or renting or investing in real estate." When you get that lead, you've actually got something. My business is over 90% by referral. Warm leads coming from real people, because I'm really contacting them.

No Leads, No Business! You Have to Prospect Every Day

Kendra Stutzman, Scottsdale, Arizona

Kendra:

Really hit the ground running with prospecting. Prospect, prospect, prospect. I make phone calls and I do lead generation three hours a day plus. Definitely get that lead generation and that database going so that you've got a lot of people to work with.

Alex Saenger:

Without leads we have no business, that's it. So how do you get leads? Well, finding and establishing a lead generation system that gives you a constant stream of business and leads coming in is the most important thing you can do. Now, where do you get most of those leads? It comes from your database. Small database, small number of leads; large database, a fountain of leads.

Make sure you build your database nice and big so you can have a steady stream of leads. And make sure that you prospect every single day.

What Thing Do You Need To Do Every Single Day?

Catherine Kelly, Morristown, New Jersey

WHAT THING DO YOU NEED TO DO EVERY SINGLE DAY?

Catherine Kelly:

You have to learn how to lead generate. That's your business. I heard that when I was a new agent, but I didn't get it … then. I didn't get the importance. They said you have two businesses as an agent, to lead generate and to be a real estate agent. And I said, "Oh, well, I just want to be a real estate agent." And the person that I was with said, "Don't worry about the leads, people just call you, it's not a big deal." And I'm going, "No." But three years into the business I understand that two, three hours a day of lead generation is where you need to be to grow your business, otherwise you're just stagnant.

Alex Saenger:

So who needs to lead generate? I mean, seriously, why would you bother? Why would you bother doing it? I mean, you don't want to grow your business do you? You don't want to double your business do you? I mean, why would you lead generate?

That's the question you have to ask yourself every morning. Because without lead generation you don't have a business. Without really understanding that lead generation is the source for doubling your database, and for increasing your revenue, you're never going to take your business to the next level. So, if you're not doing it consistently, you might want to think about it, because lead generation is probably 80% of our job.

I've talked about it before, I'll talk about it again. Lead generating. Do it right now.

Why You Need to Stay Consistent With Outreach

Barbara Best, Toronto, Ontario, Canada

Barbara Best:

I door knock four times a year with my quarterly newsletter. I postcard once a month and I do letters, so I offer something of value such as the top five reasons why you should stage your home or the top five returns on investment in terms of renovations. I'm always providing something of value. I over communicate with my farm area so that I'm always top of mind when they go to list their home.

Alex Saenger:

The whole purpose of outreach is to stay top of mind with all of the people in your database. How do you do that? Well, we've talked about in other interviews using your 36 touch. There's also using your 8 x 8 (a lead generation communication program explained in The Millionaire Real Estate Agent book by Gary Keller). What really matters is that you really focus on having a consistent way to stay in touch with those people. If you don't stay in touch with them, they're not going to think about you when it comes time to think about real estate.

Our job is to stay in touch with them. Our job is to make sure they never forget that we're in real estate. So when they know someone thinking about moving, whether it be in their local market or somewhere else, they're going to think of you because you're their real estate professional, and you want them to call you. Well, if you want that, are you staying in touch with them on a regular basis? Are you doing a 36 touch where you're emailing, snail mailing, calling, doing events, and having different things that you can invite people to? Are you staying in touch with them? If you're not doing all those things, well, get to it. That's the way you're going to build your business.

What Lead Generation Model Are You Using?

James Nellis II, Fairfax, Virginia

James Nellis II:

Consistency is hard. It's why if you look at the top 10 agents, why those names change every year. Usually, the top 10 or the top 100 agents, you'll see some of the same names, but there's a constant flow. The reason that there's a constant flow is because it depends on the lead generation model they're using.

So think back in the mid-2000s with the foreclosures and the short-sales. Those agents that focused directly on that business as their lead source, they went through the roof. There were people in the top 10 I'd never even heard of before. Guess where they are now? Foreclosures and short-sales are not a huge segment of our market in the Washington, D. C. metro area. Those people that chose to focus specifically on that, they're not in the top 10 anymore.

Alex Saenger:

So what James is talking about is top producers at a high level like him, who are doing hundreds if not literally thousands of leads or transactions a year. They struggle too, just like everybody else. The difference is, they have such high level of volume in a particular niche market that when that niche market takes a plunge, their business takes a huge plunge also.

The way you can protect your business and yourself from huge ebbs and flows is by having a consistent approach when it comes to lead generation by referral. Referrals are the number one source of lead generation across any level of business that you might see out there. So if you're wondering where you should invest your time and energy so that you don't have these big ebbs and flows, referrals is probably where you want to start.

I'm not saying that you shouldn't do some of these other things. You should, because you shouldn't just have one pillar to your business. In fact, you should have three pillars. That's why when we do a plan, we do a 1-3-5. One of those pillars is referrals. You're always going to have that as number one. Number two and number three are going to be your other plans of attack to attack the market. Two and three are the things that are going to make your business fluctuate.

If you don't have a plan put together and you don't have your database and referrals as your number one strategy, you might want to think about adding that right now.

How Time Blocking Relates to Lead Generation

Ron Goldstein, Tallahassee, Florida

Ron Goldstein:

The key, of course, is lead generation. Specifically, to focus on time blocking, designating the time to generate leads, which is the lifeblood of the business.

Alex Saenger:

What's interesting about what Ron talks about here, is that lead generation actually starts with time blocking. It's not something you naturally would think of, but if you don't consistently lead generate and you don't set aside time every day or every week to specifically lead generate, you're not going to have the activities that you need to generate the business you're looking for.

Understand that right out of the gate when you start your plan for the year or when you're sitting down at the beginning of the week trying to figure out how you're going to spend your time. Time block that time for lead generation right up front. Make it the beginning of every day or at least in the beginning of the week, to make sure that you meet your appointment goals.

178

Doing Three Hours of Lead Gen Every Morning

Luz Daniels, Englewood, Colorado

Luz Daniels:

Three hours every morning, Monday through Friday, those are my hours of lead generation. Number one, for going through with any hot leads. Anybody who has said they want to buy or sell. I'll follow up with those calls and then from there I'll call my database. I'll invite them to an event. I'll talk to them about some mailer I sent them or an email that I sent with great information that could be helpful to them. That's a way to make it about them a little bit. Find out how they're doing. How are the kids? How is the cat? How is the dog? And then remind them that we are here to help and that we're looking for business.

Alex Saenger:

Lead generation. You know, one of the things that they teach at Keller Williams is this concept of a 36 touch. A 36 touch is basically, I'm going to communicate with you, because I've met you and you know me in relation to real estate. I'm going to communicate with you 36 times a year. 12 of those might be emails. 12 of those might be snail mail, something I send you like a postcard or a newsletter in the mail, where I put a stamp on it. And then some of those things might be phone calls, like Luz was talking about. Have a consistent process that you're using to stay in touch with the people that you're actually communicating with in relation to real estate.

Make sure that you let them know, "Here's some valuable information, and, oh, by the way, I'm in real estate, and here's an event that I'm having." Or, "Oh, by the way, I'm in real estate. Here's an e-newsletter that talks about how to keep your home improved." Or maybe what's happening in the financial market, or where home sales have gone. That's the whole point of the 36 touch. Making sure that people never forget that you're in real estate, so that you can earn their referral. You can either help them or help a friend.

What Does Geographic Farming Mean?

Harry Moore, Bethesda, Maryland

WHAT DOES GEOGRAPHIC FARMING MEAN?

Harry Moore:

They told me to pick a neighborhood and farm it, because the neighborhood I lived in when I started in real estate was the outer, outer reaches of Capitol Hill. The market was terrible, so I didn't farm it. I always farmed my sphere, which has been great, but I think having a geographic farm, to really know and work, is a really strong component in any good agent's business.

Alex Saenger:

So farming. No, it's not the old guy with the straw hat and the pitch fork. That's not the kind of farming that we're talking about here. We're talking about real estate farming. We're talking about geographic farming. So what does that mean?

In geographic farming real estate, what you're focused on is a specific area. It could be a neighborhood or maybe even a zip code. A zip code is a little bit big though. Focus on a neighborhood, maybe 1,000 homes. Focus your energies and all your marketing and your attention on those 1,000 homes. You might go around and door knock some of those homes, and say, "Hey, I'm Alex Saenger. I'm your local real estate agent. I'm here to answer any questions you might have about the market." Or, "Here's a competitive market analysis just to let you know what the market is doing and what the market looks like right now."

If you're going to start farming a neighborhood, what you're going to want to do is actually get in there, meet as many people as you can, provide as much value to those people as you can, and start building a reputation as the person who is the neighborhood specialist in that local market. By doing so, you're able to have people come to you as a resource for contractors, or home improvement providers, maybe insurance, or a new roof. Whatever it is, they're going to have questions.

One of the best places to go is Nextdoor. Go to Nextdoor.com, download the app, and become a member of your local community on Nextdoor. It's a way to stay connected with the community. You could maybe sponsor neighborhood yard sales, or a shredding day, or something like that. Being involved in your community, being involved in your neighborhood, is super critical in creating a farm area. Then, once you've started marketing to those people, sending them post cards, hand written notes, making phone calls, stopping by, and knocking on the door, over time, people will start to rely on you as that neighborhood expert in that farm. Once that happens, you'll wind up generating lots of business and become the de facto person in your neighborhood.

Now, farming is very expensive because it takes time. Time is not something that new agents feel like they have. It probably takes at least two years, to really get established in a farm before you actually start generating some revenue from it.

Harry's right. Farming is a great tool in real estate, but it's a long term strategy. It's not a short term get rich quick kind of a thing. If you're thinking about a geographic farm, you should; but just know it's going to take time to turn that into profit.

What Worked Back Then Still Works Today

Nancy Bennett, Walnut Creek, California

WHAT WORKED BACK THEN STILL WORKS TODAY

Nancy Bennett:

So what worked back then, really actually works today. I was on an airplane with two of our top producers flying from San Francisco to Orlando. I was like, "Oh my, you guys made like $425,000 this year. How did you do it?" Because I was struggling. I was a little bit ego driven at that time, and the two of them sat there and said, "It's all about farming." I was like, "Farming? Seriously? I keep hearing about this farming thing. Tell me more about that." For the next six hours I just asked questions. What is farming? What does that mean? How do you connect?

I learned from them and when I came back from Family Reunion I identified a farm in my area, and started farming it consistently. Let me be very specific. Consistency. So in the next nine months I began dominating that area. There were two other agents that had been in there 15, 20 years each. I started dominating the area and I went from that farm of 1,000 people to the zip code to the city. So now, we're number one in the city of Concord for three years running.

Alex Saenger:

So while Nancy was focused on farming, what's interesting about what she said at the very beginning is that what worked a long time ago still works today. When you break real estate down into some of its most fundamental basics, relationships are how you wind up building business and getting referrals. Around 90% of my business comes by way of referral with all this technology out there. It's amazing that so much and probably more business comes by way of referral than it does from online leads and things like that.

Why? Because people use the internet to get the information they want, but they still want to deal with somebody that they trust, and the way they're going to find that person that they trust, is by recommendations from other people that they know that they trust. Not just some recommendations that they find online.

What Nancy did in her farming example, is she went into a neighborhood, but she didn't just start marketing to the people who lived there. She got involved. She got to know the people. She got to shake hands with the people. She became part of that community. Then she expanded that and expanded that again. You know what's great is, you don't have to do it yourself. If you have a team, your team members are doing it for you as well. The point is people are getting to know, not just you, but your business.

Just like you're doing right now. You're getting to learn about me and my business by the way I'm communicating with you and the expertise I have in real estate. That's part of building a relationship. So, if you're thinking about what you should be doing in your lead generation, you might want to think about, "What worked 50 years ago?" Maybe focus on that first, instead of just driving yourself to some of this new technology.

And also remember, you and I are building a relationship through this book. You are learning a lot about how I run my business and how I build relationships. And I want a relationship with you too. So send me an email or give me a call. Let's connect and exchange information. You never know when I might have a referral for you. But you will know when you have a referral for me anywhere in the Washington, D.C. metro area in Maryland, the District of Columbia, or Northern Virginia.

Being a True Community Resource

Nancy Bennett, Walnut Creek, California

Nancy Bennett:

Consistently contacting the same people over and over with a message is important. Not just, "Hey I sell homes." But "How can I help you today? How can I serve you? What resources do you need? Do you need an electrician today?"

I am also sending out information. For example, what's going on with refinance numbers, what's selling, or what's the value of a person's house. It might be asking if someone needs an appraisal for a date of death or a probate. It could be giving them information like letting them know our electrician in the middle of November is offering $45 an hour, and asking who needs his service. I let people know to give me a call, and if they do, that I'll connect them with him. So they give me a call, I get their phone number and updated information, and they're in my database. Then they get a weekly email blast or a newsletter dropped at their doorstep or a postcard or they're invited to our events.

Alex Saenger:

Be the hub. Be the center of information for all of your clients. Be the person that they go to for referrals for trade personnel like a plumber, electrician, handyman, gardener, or roofer. Whoever it is that people will need, you want to make sure that you have a network of professionals behind you that you can recommend to your clients and to your sphere. One of the ways you can find out who's looking for that information is by putting something about it in an e-newsletter to your community, or your sphere. You can put it out through a snail mail piece, or Nextdoor. If you're not a member of Nextdoor, sign up. It's free, and you can be a community leader. A lot of times people will post things on there like, "Hey, I'm looking for a babysitter." And maybe you've talked to some neighbors that have great kids that would be great babysitters and you can make a connection that way. Maybe they need a tree expert, because their tree's infected with some bugs or a disease or something like that. And you happen to have a great person that you can recommend for that. Maybe they're looking for an accountant because it's tax time. Whatever they're looking for, you want to make sure that you're in there, you're making those recommendations and you're visible to that community. You want them to reach out to you, so you can be the hub of information and you can be the one getting all the great leads for referrals.

Remember, when you give, you get …? You get leads back, and so you want to make sure that you're the person that connects your clients with great service providers and you're visible in the community doing just that.

Why Generous Real Estate Agents Are Prosperous Real Estate Agents

Laurie Satushek, Bellingham, Washington

WHY GENEROUS
REAL ESTATE AGENTS ARE
PROSPEROUS REAL ESTATE AGENTS

Laurie Satushek:

I'd probably have more events, even earlier on. I started giving away stuff very early on in my career, and that probably helped because people know. They're like, "Oh, that's awesome. Laurie's giving away pies, or Laurie does this or that." So, they know.

Alex Saenger:

In your business, coming from a place of contribution is one of the strongest positions you can take. After all, when you receive a gift from someone, do you feel maybe a little bit indebted to them?

Think about it this way. She talked about the pie. Every year we have a great pie giveaway. It's not a new concept. I didn't create it. I just use it. So, during the great pie giveaway, the Tuesday before Thanksgiving, I want people to stop in, pick up a pie, either pumpkin or apple. I give them the pie. My whole team actually dresses up as pilgrims for the event. It's great. We have the hats, the shoes, the whole thing … alright, not really. But who knows, maybe next year? Anyway, they collect the pie from me, and they go, "Wow! This is awesome. I don't have to make a pie for Thanksgiving."

Now they leave and they go, "That Alex, he was just such a great guy, and he gave us this free pie." Now, when I call them and say, "Hey, by the way, whom do you know that might be thinking about moving in the next three to six months?" They're actually going to take the time to think about it, and if they know somebody, they're going to feel like, "You know what? I'm going to go ahead and give Alex that information. I'm going to give him that referral because he's such a nice guy. He includes me. He gives me the things that I enjoy."

When you come from a place of contribution, it builds this relationship where they're not going to go anywhere else. Those people that you're communicating with and connecting with, they're receiving this information from you. They're receiving these gifts from you. They feel indebted to you. Having different events is such a great way to build that relationship. Make sure that you come from a place of contribution.

Be Open to New Methods of Lead Generation

Michele Mamo, Cincinnati, Ohio

Michele Mamo:

I think that you always have to be open to new aspects of lead generation. I built my business as a solo agent on open houses. It was great for me. It worked. But when you get moved somewhere else, you have to change your way of thinking. We had to do cold calls, we had to do for sale by owners and expired listings and practice those scripts, and we did that. We said this is a new mindset, the new way of thinking. Always open your eyes to a new way of the lead generation, because you may need it as the market shifts.

Alex Saenger:

So what works for you? Michele talks about the fact that sometimes you're going to have to think about shifting the way you do lead generation. I think back to a couple of years ago in my business. I was doing a thriving business within my farm area. My farm area produced a good amount of volume for me. I was probably making, $50, $60, $70 thousand dollars in revenue from my farm area. The issue was that the market started to shift. The demographics in the neighborhood started to shift, and the people in that neighborhood thought that they needed a different demographic profile of an agent to actually represent them.

They were wrong, because ultimately as agents, we sell to everyone. But that's not what the consumer thought. So one of the things that I needed to do, was I needed to reevaluate how much money I was spending in that farm area, and maybe redirect some of that money somewhere else. Hence, we created the Real Agent Advice videos and spent money on that instead. Communicating with viewers allowed us to build a relationship so that when they know someone thinking about moving into or out of the Washington, D.C. metro area, that they can contact me.

Likewise, people can connect with me through KWConnect, and through the referral network through KWReferrals or Kelle (the digital personal assistant from Keller Williams with artificial intelligence). That way, when I have a referral to send out, guess what? I'm going to go into that database, I'm going to find somebody, and I'm going to send that agent that referral. But had this situation with my farm area not forced me to change my direction, those steps wouldn't have been taken.

Listings Through Signs and Social Media

Julian Dixon, Kingston, Jamaica

LISTINGS THROUGH SIGNS AND SOCIAL MEDIA

Julian Dixon:

I would say number one goes to my yard sticks (signs in front of a house) and directional signs for sure, because that was number one before I even ever learned truly about lead generating from Keller Williams. That is what really got my business started. Secondly, we have learned how to lead generate using social media. I try not to make it too personal, but I still want you to be connected with my business, so I promote all my properties there, and I kind of give you an idea of what I'm doing every day in my real estate business.

Alex Saenger:

What's interesting about what Julian talks about, is she mentioned signs. Well, signs equal listings. She talks about promoting her listings on social media. When you think about it, what she's done by coming to KW, is she's defined some of the fundamental models in The Millionaire Real Estate Agent book. Of course we go back to one of our foundational models of leads, listings, and leverage, the triangle. Leads: you have to get the leads before you can get the listings. Listings is second. She's talking about the fact that listings are a critical part to her business and generating more leads. If you have a neighborhood of 200 homes and five of them are on the market and three of the signs are yours, you're probably going to get some phone calls, right?

Having those sign posts in the yard and having those directional signs spattered all over your area, are going to give you brand awareness. They will make people call you, and it's going to be the leverage you need to generate even more business, whether it be buyers or sellers. Listings are the key to your business and they're one of the foundational components of the fundamental model of The Millionaire Real Estate Agent. If you're not doing enough with listings, you might want to think about creating that section of your business, and focusing specifically on how to generate more listing leads.

I Wish I Had Been Told About Lead Generation Earlier

Gina Padro and Christine Whiteman, Garden City, New York

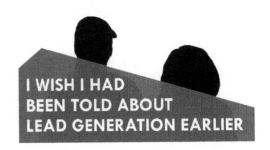

Gina Padro:

I wish I would have-

Christine Whiteman:

Lead generated.

Gina Padro:

What?

Christine Whiteman:

Lead generated.

Gina Padro:

Yes, I wish I would have known about lead generation. I would tell new agents to start with door knocking at least 200 doors a week, and doing a minimum of three open houses a weekend, because that's where you will find the buyers to generate business for yourself as a new agent.

Alex Saenger:

So, as Christine pointed out to Gina, lead generate. Lead gen, lead gen, lead gen, lead generation. One of the easiest ways for agents who don't have a database, or if they're new to an area or they don't have a very rich database, to lead generate, is to talk to other agents that have listings that are on the market, especially ones that are vacant. Talk to them, and say, "Hey, I see you have this listing. Are you planning on doing an open house this weekend?" If the answer is, "No, I wasn't," then ask, "Can I do an open house for you?" Well, of course the seller's not going to mind, the house is vacant, and they want more people through the house, because they want the house sold.

So, taking the opportunity to use that open house, and then going around the neighborhood and actually knocking on doors, and saying, "Hey, by the way, we're having an open house. It's this house down the street. It's selling for $200,000, I'd love it if you came by." Or, you could say, "Would you like to pick your neighbor? If so, let us know whom you know that might be thinking about moving into the neighborhood." Or you might say, "If you're renting, have you ever thought about buying? Maybe this would be a great opportunity for you to look at the possibility of buying a home like this one."

The point is, through that door knocking experience, you can probably pick up either a buyer or a potential seller, meaning a neighbor who's been thinking about selling but hasn't said yet, "Hey, I'm thinking about selling. Could you come and talk to me about selling a home?" So, door knocking and open houses are a great source for picking up new business for new agents.

Chapter Six:

Scripts

Introduction

Imagine you are going to have a conversation. This is an important conversation. Your business depends on it. What would you do?

Would you just walk in and try to think of what you're going to say on the spur of the moment? Or, would you learn and practice what you're going to say? If your business depended on it, you would learn and practice, right?

The thing is, you don't have to imagine these conversations. In real estate, you have these same conversations all the time. Each time you talk to a prospect or a client or another agent, you are potentially having a conversation that could impact your business. Each interaction you have could be the difference between making a sale or not. Supporting your family and living a life by design, or not.

Knowing this, you should learn and practice what to say for different real estate encounters. This isn't as hard as you might think though, because in real estate there are scripts. Scripts tell you what to say and how to say it in different real estate situations. You can learn scripts from books, online resources, and KW training. Scripts are the subject of this chapter.

In this chapter you'll learn about the importance of scripts from real estate professionals who know their value. You'll gain from their insight and be inspired to learn scripts yourself.

You learn about the importance of scripts. You'll find out how they can help you have predictable conversations, gain information, and improve your rate of conversion. You'll understand how they can help you deal with less than positive responses and how they can improve your listening.

You'll also discover that scripts can be valuable tools in your tool belt.

In a conversation where your business depends on the outcome, winging the situation isn't a good idea. Being prepared with what you need to say and how you need to say it is. Take the advice of this chapter, and know your scripts.

Why Real Professionals Always Know What They're Going to Say

Dianna Kokoszka, Austin, Texas

WHY REAL PROFESSIONALS ALWAYS KNOW WHAT THEY'RE GOING TO SAY

Dianna Kokoszka:

Learn scripts. I know agents don't like to learn scripts, because they say, "Oh it doesn't sound like me." You know what? If you haven't sold real estate, just winging it doesn't work. The reason that a magician can pull a rabbit out of a hat is because he put it in there in the first place. If you're winging it, how do you pull the rabbit out of the hat? There's no rabbit in there. You want to get the job done.

Remember, professionals absolutely know what they're going to say. Do you think an attorney walks into a courtroom without knowing what he's going to say? Do you think an actor or an actress gets on stage and doesn't know what they're going to say? The better they know what they're going to say, the more they have feelings, the more it looks and sounds like them, and they're really living the part, well guess what, those agents get paid the most.

Alex Saenger:

One thing that you want to focus on when you think about scripts is that it's a tool in your tool belt. Having lots of different tools in your tool belt and having the right tool for the right job is really important. It makes the job much easier. If you think about it that way, pulling out the tool belt, what to say when, and not having to think about what you're going to say but having that at the ready, it's so liberating to be able to do that.

You can then focus on what the other person is saying instead of what you're going to say. Dianna has really defined so many excellent world-class scripts in her coaching program called BOLD. It's something that I highly encourage anyone who hasn't taken it to take. Those that have taken it, take it again. There are people that have taken it eight, ten, twelve times that keep coming back because it's that powerful.

Making Scripts a Priority

Mary Anne Walser, Atlanta, Georgia

Mary Anne Walser:

I thought I could wing it. I'm also an attorney, so I feel like I'm very intelligent. I speak well in front of other people, but I didn't understand that there truly is a language of sales. There's a way you speak to people to get them to believe what you say. I thought that was all baloney, but it's really, really true, and scripts work.

Alex Saenger:

Mary Anne mentioned one thing that's really important, and that is the language of sales. Actually, at Keller Williams they have a course specifically just for the language of sales. It's a 10 series course. I took the course and I was blown away by some of the things that they actually had to tell me. For example, if I said to you, "Do you want to work with me?" in a down tone, or, "Do you want to work with me?" in a normal tone, or, "Would you like to work with me?" in an energetic tone, there's a difference in how you communicate. How you talk to people, what you say, and the words you use, really do make a difference.

So, if you're thinking about what you need to do next and you haven't studied scripts, you might want to get started with taking that next step.

Scripts are Vital to Your Success

Sandra Juvera, Colorado Springs, Colorado

Sandra Juvera:

Master scripts as quickly as you can, because they're vital to your success.

Alex Saenger:

So what do scripts really do for you? The question is, do you know what to say at every moment when somebody asks you a question? For example, if you were asked the question, "How's the market?" What would you normally say? Think about it. What I normally say, because I learned it from a script, is, "Well it depends. Are you buying, selling, renting or investing?" So now what happens is, they have to think about that. They have to respond and they've given me more information than I would have gotten had I just started saying, "Oh, the market's great, it's wonderful," and then started to tell them how great it is for sellers. Well, if they're looking at investing, they may not care about that. Or, if they're looking at renting they may not care about it. So understanding what they are asking and communicating with them through scripts that you've practiced is really important.

Start With Learning Your Scripts

Karen Judd, Arlington, Texas

Karen Judd:

The scripts that I need starting out are something important. They say, go and take Ignite. You go call people, but I had no idea what to say. So, what do you say right at the beginning?

Alex Saenger:

One of the fundamental things when you're starting off in any sales business is getting to know your scripts and understanding how the dialog can happen. Scripts are there to help you focus on what the other person's saying so that you can be in "listening mode" instead of thinking about what you should say to this person next.

Having great scripts, rehearsed on a regular basis, will make your job a lot easier and make you comfortable having the conversations you need to have with every one of your clients.

Use a Prelisting Lead Sheet to Create Predictable Conversations

Jayson Stone, Upper Marlboro, Maryland

Jayson Stone:

Using a seller lead sheet is important because it allows you to create predictable conversations. There's two types of people in every conversation. There's a person who dominates the conversation, because they talk the most, and then there's a person who controls the conversation, because they ask the most questions.

In the subject of seller prospecting it is really important to win the first five seconds of the call. My script would be, ring, ring, ring. "Hello." "Hi. Is this the seller of 123 Main Street?" "Uh, yes." "This is Jayson Stone calling and the reason I'm calling is because I'm the best real estate agent in town and I understand you had a dream and a goal to sell your house. Is that correct?" The answer would be yes. And this could be an expired listing, or maybe it's a withdrawn listing or even a for-sale-by-owner, or FSBO.

Now, once they've said "Yes," I have the opportunity to ask them the one sentence script and the only thing I'd have to remember from there, because everything else is on my lead sheet, "Do you have the opportunity to go over a couple of questions, because as far as I'm concerned, the proportion in which I can best help you towards that dream and goal of selling your home is directly tied to how much I know and understand about your goal? So I'd like to go ahead and ask you a couple of questions, so that I can gain that information and be of the best resource to you. May we spend some time going over that today?"

Alex Saenger:

A prelisting lead sheet is something that everyone should have when talking to a perspective seller. Now what is a prelisting lead sheet? A prelisting lead sheet is basically a script. It's a form that I fill out whenever I talk to someone who's thinking about selling a home. It really covers a lot of the basics. What's their name? What's their email address? What's the cell phone? What's the best way to get in touch with them? The first question is, "Are you already working with an agent?" Well, if they're already working with an agent, we don't want to talk to them. We can't.

"Why are you moving?" "Where are you moving to?" "How soon do you need to be there?" "What will happen if your home doesn't sell in the required amount of time?" "Relocation?" "Are you thinking of selling your home yourself?" That is such an important question. I used to never ask that question. I used to be afraid. But now I want to know if they are thinking about doing a for-sale-by-owner. Or are they just fishing for a price, or are they serious about having somebody like me sell their home.

Get information about the home. Get information about the financials. Think about that. If you knew exactly how much they were thinking about selling their home for, and you realized that what they were thinking is way off base, would you go on the listing appointment? Maybe not. You might reevaluate that conversation.

Finally, what are three things that you're expecting from your real estate agent? They're going to tell you exactly what you need to tell them, so having that information completed before you meet with them is super critical. Guess what? If you're on a team, you don't even have to do it yourself. You can get somebody else to do it for you and then you're actually reviewing these things, giving them a call, confirming your appointment, and boom … now you're in there having the appointment and you're securing that listing.

Practice Scripts to Prepare for Client Interactions

David Raesz, Austin, Texas

David Raesz:

Know your scripts. You have to be able to know how to have a conversation over the phone to set the appointment.

Alex Saenger:

Having a set of dialog that you've gone through and you've memorized to the point where you can listen to what your client is actually saying, is what a script is all about. Making sure that you're functioning as a salesperson at the highest level means that you're able to listen to what your client has to say.

Scripts are the thing that make you able to do that. Make sure that you set aside time every day, maybe half an hour or fifteen minutes for practicing scripts. Get a script partner, find somebody in your office, even somebody across the country. Practice on the phone. Practice in person.

Practicing those scripts is going to be the difference between you being an amateur and you being a professional.

What to do When a Potential Client Says No

Jayson Stone, Upper Marlboro, Maryland

WHAT TO DO WHEN A POTENTIAL CLIENT SAYS NO

Jayson Stone:

When you hear a no, that they're not ready to sign, what comes up more often than not is the fact that they just really want to go and interview more agents. That's when I ask them the turnkey question of, "Well, are you firm in meeting with all agents before you make a decision?" This is the part where you really have to have your listening ears on, because it's going to come really quick. You have to decide if they have given you an absolute yes or if there's any hesitation or maybe even a no to that question. If there's an absolute yes, they are firm they're going to meet with every real estate agent prior to making a decision, then when do you want to go? You want to go last. You want to let them have the opportunity to meet with the rest, and then they can meet with the best ... you, at the very end before making a decision.

Now, if there's any hesitation, "Well, yes we will," then I know that they're not firm and I need to go and get to that listing appointment right away, because I know that I have the opportunity to close them. If they're not firm in their resolve on meeting with everybody, it's just a surface objection.

Alex Saenger:

There's a saying that, "the skills pay the bills." The skills in this case are all about listening. It's not just about the questions that you ask and the answers that are given, but how those answers are given and the nuances in how the answers are given. If you listen carefully, you can hear a lot more than what the client or the prospect is actually saying to you.

In this case that Jayson gave, it's really a matter of figuring out, "Do I even want to go on the appointment?" Knowing how to interpret those answers and how to listen for the responses that they're giving tell us a lot more about how we want to pursue the relationship and conversation. Those skills are the things that make you an okay agent or a phenomenal agent. Make sure you brush up on your skills.

Why You Need to Requalify Your Listing Appointments

Jayson Stone, Upper Marlboro, Maryland

Jayson Stone:

We were on the subject of prequalifying our appointments. Not just prequalifying, but requalifying them before we got out to the house for the listing appointment. Prior to calling, it'd be, "Hey, Mr. and Mrs. Seller, it's Jayson. I know we have an appointment to meet tomorrow at noon. I'm just putting some final touches on our appointment." I'd get answered all the questions that I didn't get answered before. Then, before hanging up the phone, I want to make sure to ask them that magical question. Say, "If what I say makes sense to you, and you feel comfortable and confident that my team could sell your home, are you ready to list with us tomorrow?" Seeing to it that we got a positive answer to that question was critical. We wanted to know if they weren't in a position to make a decision tomorrow, to really unpack that before we got there. That is the biggest difference between mega agents, and those who are not there just yet. Mega agents go on appointments that matter. Appointments they will win.

Alex Saenger:

Setting up that listing appointment is more important than you might realize. It affects one of the characteristics in your conversion metrics for the "economic model"[10]. Now, right at the very top, we have "seller listing appointments"[11], and we have our percent "conversion rate"[12]. If you're not asking the questions Jayson's asking in his prequalification steps when he's on the phone with a client, with a prospect who's going to sell a house, your rate of conversion is going to go way down. Now, I bet you can understand that by going through the script that Jayson went through, that the percentage rate of conversion is going to be much,

---

[10, 11, 12] The Millionaire Real Estate Agent by Gary Keller with Dave Jenks and Jay Papasan. Copyright © 2004 by McGraw-Hill Education

much higher for him. If that's higher, the rest of the "economic model"[13] works even better.

So take Jayson's advice. Make sure you practice your scripts. Make sure you do your prequalification, tie down that client, and make sure you go on appointments that matter.

---

[13] The Millionaire Real Estate Agent by Gary Keller with Dave Jenks and Jay Papasan. Copyright © 2004 by McGraw-Hill Education

Chapter Seven:

Leaving Your Comfort Zone

Introduction

Some situations in real estate can be scary. They can be like standing on the end of the diving board and looking down. For some people, it might be making phone calls, for other people it might be meeting face to face. When you are a real estate professional there are many situations where you might have to leave your comfort zone.

In this chapter you'll learn about overcoming fear and being more confident. You'll find out that training, scripts, knowing your market, and learning can help.

You'll be inspired to not be afraid of uncomfortable situations, to have courage, and to take action. You'll find out about overcoming fear of rejection and learn the important lesson that failure is really progress. You'll also find out about learning from excited people.

Through the insights in this chapter, you'll gain a better understanding of conversations. You'll learn about talking on the phone, having the courage to do what others won't, interacting with people, and asking for business. You'll also find out why it's all right to talk about real estate, and you'll learn a tip from Alex for starting conversations.

Remember, real estate is about serving people. Sometimes you have to leave your comfort zone to do that, but that's all right. Learn from these professionals, and have the courage to do what you need to do.

Why People Want You to Talk to Them About Real Estate

Harry Moore, Bethesda, Maryland

Harry Moore:

Don't be afraid to talk to people about real estate. The most important skill you can learn, is to just talk to them about real estate. Most people want to talk to you about real estate. Even if you don't know everything, you can still strike up conversations and it's all about having conversations.

Alex Saenger:

Everybody loves to talk about real estate (I know I do), but how do you start the conversation? One way I start the conversation, is I wear a shirt that has my logo on it. When I wear a logoed shirt, jacket, hat, etc., it strikes up conversations. People can engage with me, without me bringing up the subject of real estate.

It's also convenient because it's just like a uniform. Every day I get up, I put on a shirt that has a logo on it and I don't have to figure out what I'm going to wear. I don't have to worry about putting on a tie (Who wants to wear a tie? There are all the colors and matching everything. There are also the knots. Do you know what a half-handed Windsor something-or-another knot is? I don't, and I don't want to tie one either). So it's really easy for me, and logoed shirts come in women's sizes too.

If you want to strike up conversations about real estate, which like Harry said, everybody needs to, just do it. That's how you get connected and how you get referrals. One of the easy ways to do it, actually a very easy and simple way, is just get something with a logo on it or put a name tag on. Whatever it is, just put something on that lets people know you're in real estate.

Have the Courage to See Failure as Progress

Mariana Costa, Centerville, Massachusetts

Mariana Costa:

I shouldn't be fearful. I shouldn't be fearful of taking action and I should just go fail. Failure's progress.

Alex Saenger:

Failure equals progress. How could that be? Because ultimately when you fail, you figure out one way of not doing something. And if you do it enough times, eventually you're going to stumble across the right way to do something. You're going to learn from your mistakes until you get it right.

Fail fast, fail often, because it's going to allow you to move your business and yourself forward in the direction that you want to head, faster.

Why Knowing Your Market Helps You to be More Confident

Gloria Frazier, Montgomery, Alabama

Gloria Frazier:

Well, a lot of times, for me, personally, I was fearful of failure. I felt like the other agents, they could do it better. Or, you know, just the competition of it. But no, educate yourself, learn your market and you can come to real estate to not just be a real estate agent. You want to help people and you want to establish your business. You want to build a business. You can't be a secret agent, and you can't be fearful. If you are, you are in the wrong field.

Alex Saenger:

So Gloria mentioned, "learn your market." If you're visiting 10 properties each week in your local market area, I guarantee you, you're going to know the inventory out there better than the person who is actually selling the house. Ultimately, knowing your market gives you the confidence you need to be able to answer questions for your client. Know what you know, know what you don't know, and then, you'll find out that you're going to be able to get all the answers that you need to give to your clients. They're going to trust you because you're not trying to snowball them and tell them something that's not true. You're going to tell them the truth, you're going to tell them what you know. You're going to give them your experience and when you don't know something, you're going to double check.

Don't be Afraid of the Telephone

Tom Harmon, Frisco, Colorado

DON'T BE AFRAID OF THE TELEPHONE

Tom Harmon:

Don't be afraid of the telephone. You have to use it all the time. You can't do everything on the internet. You have to get face to face with people and talk to them.

Alex Saenger:

In the end, real estate is about contact. It's something that requires you to get on the phone and actually have conversations with people. Make sure that you get in touch with them, either by phone or face to face. Those interactions allow you to build rapport and build a relationship with people that builds trust and allows them to send you referrals. Without that relationship, there's no way they're going to send you a referral. Make sure that you get in touch with people, call them, have coffee, have different events, and make sure you're actually interacting with them face to face.

Facing the Fear of Rejection

Catherine Kelly, Morristown, New Jersey

FACING
THE FEAR
OF REJECTION

Catherine Kelly:

The greatest thing that you have to get over is fear of rejection. I heard something, and I've heard it reinforced time and time again, that when somebody objects to you, when somebody gives you an answer back that you don't want to hear, they're not rejecting you. They want to work with you. That's the key, because if they didn't say anything back, it means they didn't care, and they'd walk away, and they don't want to work with you. So, objections are not a bad thing, just like, "no," is not a bad thing.

Alex Saenger:

Objections are just another way for people to actually engage with you and to have a conversation with you. They're giving you the opportunity to overcome that objection and to win them over. When you do, you'll find that those people actually become your greatest advocates. Don't be afraid of no. Don't be afraid of rejections. They are an opportunity for you to win a new client.

Fears About the Business Will Lessen With Training

Maria Hurtado, Yuma, Arizona

Maria Hurtado:

They're scared because of the unknown. Being with Keller Williams is an education. It's being educated and knowledgeable. I think that's what we're more afraid of, not knowing the unknown. But once you know what to do and how to do it, then you'll become successful.

Alex Saenger:

So what's interesting about what Maria's talking about, if you drill down on facing your fears, it comes down to one thing and that's training. Training equals confidence and training equals success. Because the more you're trained, the better you're going to do. If you are uncomfortable with what you're supposed to say, train with scripts because the scripts are going to give you the confidence to know what to say when, so you won't have to think, "Oh, what am I supposed to say?" You'll just know automatically what to say.

So to face your fears and to get the confidence you need to be excellent at this job of real estate, go get the training.

Create Success by Doing the Things That Others Won't

Jackie McKelvin, Littleton, Colorado

CREATE SUCCESS BY DOING THE THINGS THAT OTHERS WON'T

Jackie McKelvin:

I would just say, commit to doing what most people are not willing to do, so you can have what most people don't have. Those are some of the things I always tell myself. When I face something that was kind of tough, either a tough phone call or maybe calling someone that I was intimidated by, I just hit dial. That courage will show up. That knowledge will just show up. Just do it, because if you stop short, you're doing what most people are doing. They're stopping, and they don't have what most people want to have. And so, I think that was a big thing for me.

Alex Saenger:

What Jackie's talking about is having the courage to do the things that other people won't do. Let's say you're afraid of making phone calls. You're afraid of calling that person that you know about real estate. But if other agents had that courage to call that person, they would have beat you to it, right? But if you're the one that actually makes that phone call, you're the one that has that conversation with that person first. You might be the only one that ever has had that conversation.

If you have the courage to make the phone call and you have the courage to do the things that other people won't do, you, in turn, will get rewarded. You will be rewarded with building a deeper relationship with those people. And you'll be the one that they decide to do business with, once they decide they actually want to buy or sell a house.

So, have some courage. And do the things other people won't do.

How Learning Scripts Can Help You to Get Out of Your Comfort Zone

Heather Murphy, Concord, Massachusetts

Heather Murphy:

Being uncomfortable is something that comes to mind. I think that I wish someone had told me that pushing myself to be uncomfortable, to get contacts and leads and ask for them, was something I should do. I wish someone had told me that you don't necessarily have to do phone calls all the time. It's kind of finding what's best for your approach, for who you are and going after that in conjunction with being uncomfortable.

Alex Saenger:

What Heather's talking about here in terms of leaving your comfort zone, for her, it was asking for the business. For a lot of people, it's asking for the business, myself included. I wasn't always somebody that could just go up and ask somebody for business. Over time, I didn't just learn the script, I made it part of who I am.

Really leaving your comfort zone is actually about learning your script. If I asked you right now, if we had a conversation, and I just say, "By the way, really quick, before we leave, whom do you know that might be thinking about moving in the next three to six months?" That's not an uncomfortable question for me to ask and it sounds very natural, well I hope anyway.

Practicing my scripts over and over, gave me the ability to be more confident about asking the question and facing that possibility of rejection. It's also the way you ask the question. So understanding your script will allow you to make it part of your comfort zone and it'll allow you to push yourself to be more successful.

Real Estate Isn't About You

Michael Acquisto, San Antonio, Texas

Michael Acquisto:

I spent thirty years as a telephone company employee that worked in an office. I didn't have any reason to get outside of myself. I wish they would have showed me how I can be of help to other people and not internalize everything. I wish they would have told me it wasn't about me. It wasn't those people coming to me to provide them a service, it was me going to them to be of service.

Alex Saenger:

They always say that you are given two ears and one mouth because that's how much you're supposed to listen compared to how much you're supposed to talk. This is an important lesson for any agent to learn.

When your clients get in touch with you, they're looking to you because of your professionalism. They're looking to you to give them guidance and advice. They're looking for something from you, but not you yourself. They are not coming to you because you are great, but because what you can do is great.

Your clients want you to focus on them and articulate the guidance and advice you have. They want you also to affirm what they're thinking. Make sure that when you talk with your clients, you tell them back what you heard from them to make sure you're on the same page. The only way you can do this is if you listen more than you talk, and realize the interaction is about them and not yourself.

You have a lot of experience to share and can give great advice. You have to remember though, the only way you can give this advice is if you focus on the client before yourself.

Surround Yourself With People That Want to Grow

Alisa Parrent, Anchorage, Alaska

Alisa Parrent:

> I wish somebody would've said how important it is to just go outside of your box of learning and be surrounded with people that are in that same excitement level and have the ability to want to grow like everybody else.

Alex Saenger:

> So what Alisa's talking about here is surrounding yourself with people that are excited to grow, people that are excited to learn, and people that are excited to just expand their horizons and expand what they're capable of doing. I don't know about you, but I would much rather be around people who are excited to learn and excited about what they're doing, rather than people who have been doing it for a long time and are kind of humble and content with where they are, and are not really looking to grow and expand

> At Keller Williams, one of the reasons people come to Keller Williams is because they're looking to grow their business. They're looking to take their business to another level. By surrounding yourself with other people that want to grow, you yourself will grow automatically. Almost guaranteed. If you're thinking about Keller Williams and you're not sure but you know you want to grow your business, I would definitely say give us a call.

Putting Yourself Out There

Harrison Beacher, Washington, D.C.

Harrison Beacher:

When I first got into the business, I wish somebody would have told me to take more action. I spent a lot of time kind of looking at things and just analyzing, saying things like, "Oh, what are these top folks doing? I can't do that." I was just limiting my belief that I couldn't get to those levels of production. Whereas, had I early on just taken more consistent action in terms of door knocking, working my sphere, or something early on, it would have, I think, put me in a better position.

Alex Saenger:

So what Harrison's talking about is, don't get stuck with analysis paralysis. Stop analyzing everything and get busy doing stuff.

If you don't put yourself out there, nobody's going to know you're even in the business. Make a plan, even if it's a small one, execute it and be consistent. That's the way you're going to get business and that's what, getting out there, is going to win you more clients.

Chapter Eight:

Clients First

Introduction

A lot of businesses talk about putting customers or clients first. They might have signs on their walls about it and it could be something they tell their employees. Have you ever thought though, what does putting clients first look like?

What does it look like when "the customer is number one"? What does it look like when a business really provides great customer service?

In this chapter, real estate professionals give you their perspective on putting clients first.

You'll learn the importance of providing great customer service. You'll learn you can do this by solving problems for them and listening to what they have to say. You'll find out about admitting mistakes to your clients, following through on your commitments, letting your clients know if you don't know something, and the importance of caring about your clients more than your commission. The lessons of being transparent, honest and trustworthy, as well as the age old advice of treating people the way you want to be treated, will be reinforced.

You'll also read about examples of client appreciation events and doing unexpected things for your clients and you'll find out why your role is really to educate your clients.

Remember, your clients are your business. Without your clients, you have no business. When you focus on client needs, really put the customer first, and care for your clients, those clients will become a referral source for you and help your business grow.

Read on to find out how you can put your clients first.

The First Thing is Clients First

JoAnn Callaway, Scottsdale, Arizona

JoAnn Callaway:

The first thing of course is clients first. I wish they'd have told me how I could've done what I've done early on, but I didn't know that. Now I know, clients first. That takes us to the top.

Alex Saenger:

When I work with clients, it doesn't matter to me whether they buy, sell, rent or invest. What matters to me is that I serve them and give them the best possible experience, and then educate them through the process. If I've done that, I've done my job and I know that even if they don't do anything at all, I'm still going to get a referral from them.

Putting your clients first is the thing that's going to give you longevity in your business, and it's the right thing to do, because after all, it's how you'd want to be treated.

Prioritize the Client Over Everything

Mercedes French, Huntington Beach, California

Mercedes French:

It's really, really important, especially for new agents, to realize that the client has to come first. This is a people business. You're making decisions for people that involve hundreds of thousands of dollars or helping them make the decisions. These are peoples' homes. This is where people go to get away from it all. This is the roof over their head. Do the right thing by the client, and good things will follow.

Alex Saenger:

Many years back, probably 10 or 15 years, I had someone contact me. It was a sad situation. It was a young mother who had twin babies and an older toddler, and her husband passed away. She was a widow and she needed to settle the estate. When she did that, she contacted me, not to sell her house, but because she was interested in finding out what her house was worth, so that the estate could establish a baseline.

Fast forward eight years later, and she winds up talking to one of her friends about what I had done for her. Her friend contacted me, and said, "Hey, we've got this townhouse and we'd love you to sell it. Oh, by the way, we want to buy a single-family home." Because that one little act of kindness and one little act of empathy helped her at her time of need, several years later, she wound up sending me about one and a half million dollars of business, just because of that little thing that I did for her a long time ago. And it was something I wanted to do.

Listening to and Understanding Your Clients

Michael Routh, Edwards, Colorado

Michael Routh:

It doesn't matter who the client is or what their background is, they're all looking for one thing, and that's your personalized attention. Listen to them, ask them questions, and find out how you can serve them.

Alex Saenger:

So what Michael's talking about is taking the time to really understand and listen to your clients. One of the things that I do when I meet with my buyers in particular, is I actually have a guide for going through their home. It's a questionnaire that has over 70 questions. The wonderful thing about this is, it allows me not to talk, but to listen, and to give them the personalized attention that they're looking for and deserve.

Ultimately, whatever they tell me, I'm going to write down and I'm going to repeat back to them, because they want to be affirmed. They want to know that you're listening to them and giving them that personal attention. It all starts with having the conversation and understanding their needs. From there, we make a priority list and then go find them the perfect home.

Treat Customers the Way You Would Want to be Treated

Susan Buchman, Albuquerque, New Mexico

Susan Buchman:

I think that customer service is number one. Honesty and treating people the way you'd like to be treated. I think I am a social butterfly. I love working with people. I love helping people. I think understanding and listening to their needs, so that I can fine tune what it is that they're looking for, and/or listening to provide them the service that they're looking for, is also important.

Alex Saenger:

In the world that we live in, customer care obviously is super important. Customer care starts with honesty and trustworthiness because when you serve your clients and you give them the service that they're looking for, it starts with giving them honest answers to the questions that they're asking. After all, it's how you would want to be treated. So that's what you want to do for them. By providing that level of care and that level of customer satisfaction, not only are you going to take care of their transaction and take care of their needs, but they're going to wind up sending you referrals because of it.

Care More About Your Clients Than You do About Your Commission

Heather Murphy, Concord, Massachusetts

Heather Murphy:

Caring about your clients more than your commission and being able to be the resource for anything and everything that they need from the very, very, very beginning before they even, maybe even think, they're going to buy or sell, until 20 years later, is very important.

Alex Saenger:

How does that show up in your business?

Heather Murphy:

I think it's about details. It's about the little extra things that I do just to make sure my clients are extremely happy and feel as though they don't need to worry about anything. All they need to do is call me, ask me, and we will solve the problem.

Alex Saenger:

Customer care is about solving problems. As a real estate agent, you might think that you sell homes for a living, but in fact, we actually solve problems for a living. That's not something a lot of people think about when they think about getting into real estate. Every single transaction has its challenges; every single transaction is different. One time it might be a loan issue, another time it might be a home inspection issue. Our job is to help the other agent, the buyer, and the seller keep the transaction together and get it to closing for our clients.

Always be Straight With Your Clients

Dalia "Dee Dee" Cortez, Corpus Christi, Texas

Dalia "Dee Dee" Cortez:

You want to make sure that you make it as easy as you can for the seller or the buyer. Make sure you're there when they need you, answer their questions to the best of your ability, and if you can't do that, make sure you let them know, "I don't know, but I'll find out." And I will admit it, after 30 years, I can admit I don't know it all. So I still will say, "I don't know the answer. I'll find out and I'll give you a call back on it."

Alex Saenger:

Customer care is about caring for your clients. Not lying to them. Not telling them something that you don't know. Not making something up, but actually genuinely caring enough for them to tell them, "You know what? I need to double check on that." Or, "You know what? I have no idea, but I am going to find out, because you're that important to me, and I'm going to make sure I get you the information."

Or better yet, "You know what? I know somebody who would know a better answer to that question than I do. Let me check with that person and then let me get back to you." Isn't that what you would want if you were the one on the receiving end of the information? It probably is. So make sure you tell people, if you don't know the answer, that you're going to find out for them.

If You Make a Mistake With a Client Just Admit It

Luz Daniels, Englewood, Colorado

IF YOU MAKE A MISTAKE WITH A CLIENT JUST ADMIT IT

Luz Daniels:

Always follow through. When you tell your client that you're going to do something, do it. If you mess up for some reason and don't get it done, call them. If you have promised, for example, a CMA by a certain day, and it isn't done, call them. If you have promised to connect them with a lender, and you can't, call them. With any promises you make, or anything that you offer, if you can't do it, people understand. They understand that we are humans and we make mistakes, or life happens, or events happen, or anything. Just let them know what happened and make sure you get done what you said you would.

Alex Saenger:

Let me ask you, have there ever been people in your life that didn't keep their promises? Maybe they didn't follow through on something they told you they would do? How did it make you feel? Did they call and say, "Oh, my. You know what? I'm so sorry. I meant to do this." Before they called and said they were sorry, you thought they were such bad people. But after they called and explained to you what was going on, you thought, "You know what? I can understand that. They're human. They're just like me. They make mistakes. Things get in the way. Life gets in the way. Their family gets in the way. Their spouse gets in the way."

Understand that other people know that you're just a person like them and that you can make mistakes and that it's okay. But more importantly, if you make a commitment to deliver something, if you make a commitment at a listing appointment that you're going to get back in touch with them the next day, just make sure you do it. If you don't, there has to be a good reason and make sure you apologize for that. Own it. If you are in good communication with your clients or your prospects, they're going to respect that, and they're going to respect that you're human and that you have situations too. You're not going to be able to solve every problem. You're not going to be able to salvage every relationship. As long as you understand that going in, you'll be fine.

Be Transparent But Pick Your Words Wisely

Dalia "Dee Dee" Cortez, Corpus Christi, Texas

BE TRANSPARENT BUT PICK YOUR WORDS WISELY

Dalia "Dee Dee" Cortez:

It's important that you are as transparent as you can be with that buyer or that seller, because remember, you work for them. Depending on the situation, if you sign as a buyer's representative or you're listing that property, you're working for them, so you need to be as transparent as you can.

What I mean by transparent, is being as honest as you can and showing them the numbers. You show them a true CMA (comparative market analysis), for example, on the seller's side, and listen to what they're telling you, because most of the time they will say, "Well my house is worth this much." But if they look at the numbers, then you can make them understand.

When it comes to the buyer's side, you have to also do a CMA and you show them, "Okay, this is what this area's selling for. You need to be right within what sells." Because like anybody else, you try to make offers and sometimes they're so low, the seller gets offended to where they don't want to work with you. But if you teach your buyer, then it should be a smooth transaction.

Alex Saenger:

Dee Dee's talking about two separate things. The first is how you communicate with your client. What phrasing you use, "trust me", things like that. One of the things I cannot stand is when people say, "To be honest with you," and then they start telling you something. Because when someone says, "To be honest with you," it implies that everything else they have said to you is a lie. "It's only now, right at this point in the conversation that I finally decided to, "be honest with you."" I actually had to coach one of my clients, who's also in sales, to stop saying that. He would say it every other word, and it bothered me.

Now second, she talked about educating her client when it came to the market. One of the best things that you can do, one of the things I do, is I actually will bring my sellers into my office. When I go visit with them to see their house on a listing appointment, I do not talk about price and I do not talk about commission. What I do is, I have them come into the office after I've met with them at their home and had a chance to see what it is they are selling.

When we're in the office, I pull information up on the big screen, because we have a big television in our office that I can plug my computer into. I show them on the big screen all the comparable homes that I've researched that compare to their property, that are in the neighborhood, or nearby with similar features or similar prices.

And we'll go through each one of those, picture by picture, and we'll actually look and see, "How does this kitchen compare to yours? How does this bathroom compare to yours? How does this yard compare to yours? How does this floor plan compare to yours?"

With every single one of those houses we go through, they're going to have a very clear picture that, "You know, that kitchen's way nicer than mine," or, "My kitchen is way nicer than that one."

It's going to give us a level playing field so that when we have the conversation about at what price to list the house, we're going to wind up really narrowing down the actual price.

Those are some of my tips for listing presentations and for how to communicate with your client.

Unique Client Event

Barbara Best, Toronto, Ontario, Canada

Barbara Best:

One thing I do is, I focus mostly on listings. I do a client appreciation event twice a year. I actually have it on the terrace of my own condo. A lot of my clients are downsizing, so I say if you want to know what it's like to move into a smaller space or a condo, why don't you come to my client appreciation event. I have it totally catered. It's wine and full bar. I always get probably about 60 to 80 people there, and it's awesome.

Alex Saenger:

You may know about the 36 touch – communicating with each of the people in your database 36 times per year. One of the cornerstones behind any really good 36 touch program to stay in touch with your past clients, or the people in your database, is client appreciation events. I like to use them. I typically have four in a year, because it gives me an opportunity to send clients an invitation in the mail, send them an email invitation, send them a reminder email invitation, and make a phone call. I also usually do a video message or two. That's four plus touches before an event even starts, and then if they actually register for the event, reminding them, 'Hey, it's coming up tomorrow. Don't forget.' Then there is one more touch, thanking them for actually participating. For people that have actually communicated and participated, wow, it's a super high return in terms of the number of touches we can get.

What are some client appreciation events? Barbara talked about hosting something at her own place of residence. For me, that's not going to work (I generally have events at my office). It's not going to work for my family, but for her, it did. That's the kind of relationship she has with her clients. Quite frankly, she's in control over that because it's her place. It doesn't matter where you have an event, as long as it's a place that works for you.

Among the other things that I've done in the past, one of best things that you'll see across the nation, is the great pie giveaway. That's where you give them a pie at Thanksgiving time. Other types of things people have are hayrides or barbecues. You might have a water event if you have a nearby lake or pool or something similar. You might have a bowling night where you rent out the bowling alley, or a movie night where you rent out the movie theater.

Now, if you're a smaller agent, what I like to do is get together with a bunch of other agents in the office, and have an event that is, for example, our great pie giveaway, which we have here in the office. I invite all the agents in the office to participate. Why? Because even if I only have three people that show up (I usually have quite a crowd though), then if I have three, and another person has three, and yet another person has three, all of a sudden, you have five agents that have three guests each, and now there are 15 guests, plus the five agents. All of a sudden, there are 20 people, plus their families. Wow, that's actually an event.

Keep in mind, with client appreciation events, it's not actually about how many people show up at the event. Rather, it's how many people you communicate with about the event. I would imagine that when you get invited to something, you think to yourself, "That was nice. They thought of me. That was really nice of them to actually invite me to that event, even though I can't go." And that is exactly how you want the people in your database to think of you, right?

What Unexpected Thing do You do for Your Clients?

Jason Van Stiphout, Oshawa, Ontario, Canada

Jason Van Stiphout:

One of the things I do for my buyers and for my sellers, is I have four moving trailers. So when you buy and sell with me, you get moved for free. You load it up, I drive it back, put it in your driveway, and your guys unload. Second, one thing I do with a lot of my buyers and sellers, depending on who they are, is we do a backyard dinner party. I get their 10 closest friends, and I actually do all the cooking. My team helps serve, so it's a very personal experience.

Alex Saenger:

How cool is that? He actually will drop a trailer off in your driveway or in front of your house. You pile it up and he'll drive it over to the next house. That's some pretty serious customer service. That's hands-on customer service, just like getting in there, and cooking a dinner for people. The great thing is, he's absolutely right. This is going to be something nobody's going to forget. If you're really awesome, and if you're a really great chef, they're never going to forget what a great meal they had. If you're not so good … that's also something they're not going to forget.

It doesn't matter what it is, whatever it is that makes you unique, and gives you an opportunity to provide your clients with an unexpected extra, to go that extra mile to make yourself stand out, that's the thing that they're going to remember and that they're going to tell all their friends about. You know that Jason's clients are telling people about the fact that he brought them a trailer, and he delivered it to the next house. You know that his clients that are having that intimate dinner party are talking about how their agent did this wonderful experience serving them dinner at their new home, in their backyard.

I guarantee you anybody else they talk to, they're not having that same conversation about their agent. So, what are you going to do? What's your unique proposition? What's your unique unexpected extra that you're going to provide to your clients? I know what mine is. Do you know what yours is?

Wouldn't You Want Your Real Estate Agent to Treat You Well?

Catherine Delf, Latham, New York

Catherine Delf:

In real estate, we're all about the service we provide. I think providing topnotch customer service and making sure that your clients have a really great experience when they work with you is just the most important thing.

Alex Saenger:

Let me ask you, do you like great customer service? It's pretty much a yes or no answer. I'm guessing you're going to say yes, you do like great customer service. Guess what? So do your clients. Let me ask you, if you give your clients great customer service, do you think that they're going to recommend you? I would say yes, right? Ultimately, customer care is probably one of the most important things that you can do, other than lead generation, other than knowing real estate. Making sure that you take care of your clients is very important. You give them a great experience. You educate them through the process. And you then give them some unexpected extras.

In the end they say, "Wow. That was a great experience. I'd love to give you a referral. I'd love to give you a recommendation online." But make sure you ask for those reviews. Make sure you ask for a video testimonial. Because when they have a great experience, you want them to share with everybody they can and guess what? Sometimes you have to ask. Sometimes you ask for that referral. Sometimes you ask for that recommendation or that review online. It's okay to do that, because if you're giving great customer care and a great customer experience, you deserve to get that recognition publicly.

Guess what? If you don't ask, you don't get.

Chapter Nine:

Being Part of a Team

Introduction

Go team! Go team! T – E – A – M! Go Team!

All right, real estate isn't a sporting event, but teams in real estate are so important that they should be cheered for. Joining a team or building one can be important steps in the success of your business.

If you are just starting out in real estate, a great piece of advice that you will learn from this chapter is to think about joining a team. And the earlier the better.

Joining a team gives you the ability to learn from others. It gives you the ability to get the benefit of years of experience. It gives you a chance to ask people questions and bounce ideas off them. It also gives you the opportunity to experience more transactions in a given time period than you would on your own. Being on a team is something you should do sooner rather than later and it is a great way to learn about the business.

If you are thinking of growing a team, one piece of advice you'll get from this chapter, is to do it sooner rather than later. You'll learn to make sure to hire talented people and make sure to vet them properly, but you'll also learn that you should hire them as soon as you can.

In the chapter you'll also learn about the importance of hiring that first assistant or administrative person. You'll learn how this person can actually cost less than someone whom you pay commission, despite the fixed cost, and how this person can take care of tasks you don't want to handle and free you up for the more important work of your business. You'll learn that the administrative role is an important one for you to fill.

When you do decide to have team members, there are several things you need to do to be successful. In this chapter, you'll learn about helping team members achieve their goals (which can help you achieve your own at a higher level), expecting results from team members, making sure your team follows your values and standards, and holding team members accountable.

This chapter also talks about a number of benefits that having a team can bring to you besides what's described above. You'll learn how a team can help you manage volume and grow. You'll learn about how a team helps you leverage yourself. And you'll also learn how having a team can give you the ability to take a break, take a vacation, and even retire.

If you're not on a team, you should think about joining one. If you are thinking of growing your own team, you should do so as soon as you are able. If you have a team, manage your team members the right way to help your business succeed.

Go Team!

Top Producers Say They Would Have Joined Teams Sooner

Nancy Bennett, Walnut Creek, California

Nancy Bennett:

Getting on a team, was not an option when I was starting out. If you could get on a team for two to five years, and learn from that person that has made tons of mistakes, that has established a path to success and learn not only how to be a buyer's agent or how to be a listing agent, or how to make calls, or how to be in operations, but also how to look at the vision and understand the market and the network, and profit and loss statements, and so forth ... If I had that, I would have joined a team and just been a sponge. Really. And maybe ran their team, or maybe gone off and built my own team. Does that make sense?

But the opportunity to learn from somebody else is invaluable. So, we're blessed with mentorship, but joining a team is like a mentorship on steroids. It's being a part of something bigger, even if it's only two people or five people. And just having somebody to hold you a little bit accountable on a daily basis as opposed to saying, "Hey, I'm sitting in my house. Let me just go get that load of laundry going, and then I'm going to come back and then I'm going to start my calls. Then I'm going to work on my newsletter." Having somebody in the next cube going, "Wow, you know what? I just got off the phone with this guy and here's my issue. What would you have done differently or better?"

Having that is important. That's what we try and do on our teams. It's comradery. It's accountability. It's bouncing ideas off of each other. "Am I thinking strangely, or should we do this?" Right? And, "Do we want to commit dollars and maybe take it away from this program and put it towards this?" Yes, being part of a team is important.

Alex Saenger:

So what's interesting about this particular interview, is I've talked to a lot of really successful real estate agents who have built teams over the years. What's really interesting is that when you ask them the question, "If you had to do it all over again, what would you change?" Every single one of those really overly successful agents has said, "I would have joined a team right from the start." Sure, there's Productivity Coaching, there're mentorships, and there's regular coaching. They are not the same thing though as being day in and day out on a team, and being able to talk to and interact with those people that have done it before you and that have built a successful business. There's almost no better way in real estate to get started than learning from those people.

We were talking in our office the other day about how when people get their license at first, they really should be in some sort of internship before they really go out into the world because, let's face it, you might be 40 years old and you just got your real estate license – yes, you've got life experience, but you don't know anything about how to buy or sell a house, or how to advise a client on how to do that. So don't you think you should have somebody behind you backing you up, not just a team leader or a manager? You should be part of an organization that has people to do that. If you're just new in real estate and you're thinking about joining a team, I would strongly encourage you to do that.

Why Joining A Team Can Fast Track Your Education

Barbara Best and Jason Van Stiphout, Ontario, Canada

Barbara Best:

If I was starting over, even from the job that I came from to real estate, I would 100% start on a team or with a mentorship program. I would do it for a year because it'll propel your career so much faster than trying to do it on your own or just going to courses on your own. I spent probably three to four years trying to figure everything out. If I had a …

Jason Van Stiphout:

Coach.

Barbara Best:

Yes, exactly.

Jason Van Stiphout:

They're going to show you the tricks and traits and are going to keep you accountable. And that's probably one of the biggest failures for people too, keeping yourself accountable.

Barbara Best:

I'd also say don't worry about the splits when going on a team, and worrying about if someone's going to take advantage of you and all that because a lot of people talk about that. Just spend that year thinking about it as an apprenticeship. Don't worry about the money. The money will come. It will come.

Alex Saenger:

When you get into business, you can go through the Ignite program which is a basic training, if you will, for real estate agents. You can go into Productivity Coaching, which is a fantastic approach to getting you launched in the business, and you can go into a mentorship program where you look up to another agent who's actually going to help you through your first few transactions. Then you're kind of on your own. Unless, you wind up having a coach.

Now, the difference between that and joining a team is that joining a team gives you all of that combined in one, where you have a more concentrated relationship with the team leader and the rest of the members of the team. It gives you an accelerated path to learning and making money fast. It gives you the opportunity to work with some business that maybe other people aren't interested in. Yes, you're not going to get the same split as if you had gone off and done it on your own, but what's more important is you're going to get more business and more transactions faster. You're going to learn the ropes in terms of how to generate those leads, how to write a contract, how to negotiate a contract, and maybe even do a listing. You're going to learn those ropes much faster than if you tried it on your own. And while you might make, let's say half the money you would than if you did it on your own, you're going to get probably five times as much business by doing it that way, and your expenses will be substantially reduced.

Why You Don't Have to do it Alone

Joanne Curtin, Roswell, Georgia

Joanne Curtin:

Well, the big one for me, right when I got into the business, I bought a real estate book that was ridiculously not informative for what I needed. That was disappointing. Everyone told me that I didn't need to look into other things other than just learn how to do it myself. I wished they had said something else or encouraged me, because I did want to join forces with some other agent. They encouraged me to do it on my own. I wish that people would have said, "You know what? Join a team. Get in business with other real estate agents."

Alex Saenger:

There are many different ways to do real estate. You can be a solo agent, you can find a partner and be a duo, or you can build a team and you can work with a group of people all with the same goal in mind. In most cases, the most successful path, in terms of the highest number of units and the highest number of dollar value that you're selling, is going to be with a team.

There are some agents that are just exceptional individuals, and they have a high level of achievement by themselves, and they can do great business and be successful by "going it alone." The problem with that is, what happens when you want to go on vacation? What happens when you need a break? What happens when you need help? It's really hard to do it alone.

That's what Joanne was talking about. Sometimes making sure that you're with someone else in real estate is very important, because it allows you to be more flexible with your time and it allows you to specialize on the aspects of real estate that you're most interested in.

242

Achieving More by Expanding Your Team

Lauren Donnelly, Washington, D.C.

Lauren Donnelly:

I need to buckle down and just suck it up and know that I'm going to have to focus on hiring somebody. Even though I don't really want to have to worry about it, it's necessary for growth. I might as well just jump into it, suck it up, and reap the rewards sooner rather than later.

Alex Saenger:

One of the things that Lauren talks about is, working by yourself, or even if you have people working for you, eventually we all run into a ceiling of ability. In fact, Gary Keller's The Millionaire Real Estate Agent book has a discussion about breaking through a higher level of achievement. And a lot of times a breakthrough is in the form of another asset, another team member that you can leverage to help you break through that level of achievement and get to yet another level of achievement. In fact, breaking through that next level of achievement is often times not a matter of what to do, but whom to hire.

In fact, when I joined Keller Williams, I was at about $7 million in volume. When I joined here, I broke through that level and went to $10 million. Then the next year, $13 million. So I was able to almost double my business in about two years by breaking through that level of achievement by hiring excellent talent.

Don't Let Someone With Talent Pass You By

Michael Routh, Edwards, Colorado

DON'T LET SOMEONE WITH TALENT PASS YOU BY

Michael Routh:

I run a team, so allowing your team to do the job you've hired them to do is important. Don't take back the jobs that you hired somebody for. Seek out talent and always find a place for them on your team. If somebody walks into your life and you're thinking, "I wish they were in business with me," find a way to put them in the business with you.

Alex Saenger:

Talent is one of those words that we just love. Talent shows on television, talent shows at the high school. Talent shows are also for real estate. If you're building a team, you're looking for talent. You want to have great people around you that are better at things than you are. Otherwise, why keep them around? If you give somebody a job and that person does not do it well and you have to do it, should you have that person around? Maybe not. You should probably let that person go.

Giving somebody a task and having that person excel at that task and actually take it beyond where you would have taken it yourself, that's talent. One of the things that I do here in our local market center, is I teach Ignite. Ignite is a class for new agents or more junior agents that are still learning the business. What it allows me to do is give the information to a group of people, watch how they're receiving it, see how they're actually reacting to it, and the kinds of questions they're asking.

When you look at that and you see who is actually doing their homework, and they're coming back the next day, and they've visited 10 properties, knocked on 10 doors, made 10 phone calls and sent out 10 note cards, guess what? That's probably somebody that's going to go somewhere. That person is probably talented. That might be somebody I might want as a buyer's agent on my team.

If you're thinking about building a team, look for talent, look for people that can do things better than you can and that are going to push your business forward.

Why You Should Choose Your Team Members Wisely

Laurie Satushek, Bellingham, Washington

WHY YOU
SHOULD CHOOSE
YOUR TEAM MEMBERS WISELY

Laurie Satushek:

You know, to tell you the truth, right off the bat, I just tried a whole bunch of different things. And I think that was an asset. I was like, "Okay, I'll try this. I'll try that." But I didn't take Recruit Select (also known as Career Visioning, a course that teaches you how to recruit talent through KW). So as far as hiring good people, I just let people come to me. And I was like, "Oh, it's great they want to work with me." But now, I select who I want to work with me.

I will only take people that come from contribution, that are givers, that are hard workers, and that I know will always have clients' interests first. So, I trust the process, and that's why it's really important to have good people that work for me, because I've had to fire a few people that didn't come from contribution. There's givers and takers in the world, and I will only surround myself with givers in this business, for me.

Alex Saenger:

Hiring the right people, is critical to making your team as successful as possible. Just because you know some people, and you like them, doesn't necessarily mean that they're the perfect fit for the roles you're looking to fill. Ultimately, when you're thinking about hiring somebody, number one, you might want to look to hire a professional to help you with that process. It's not as easy as you might think. After all, when I hired my last assistant, I actually hired a recruiter to find exactly the right person.

That person wound up relocating from out of state to come and join my team. In the end, we wound up doing a Keller Personality Assessment, or a KPA. We wound up doing a DISC Profile like Tony Robbins has. And we even did How to Fascinate by Sally Hogshead. That tool has different personality assessments that allow you to understand how that person thinks, how you think, and if there's going to be a good match between the two of you.

245

It's not just whom you like, but as Laurie mentions, it's finding people that come from contribution, and making sure that there's a good natural fit between what they're capable of doing, and what your needs are on your team.

Expand Your Team to Manage Volume

Barbara and Lee Potts, Kahului, Maui, Hawaii

EXPAND YOUR TEAM TO MANAGE VOLUME

Barbara Potts:

Building a team is important because we've been at the point where we have more clients than Lee and I can handle. Building a team and making sure that the team is working within our value structure and the standards that we set is important for us.

Lee Potts:

Yes, our culture.

Barbara Potts:

Yes.

Lee Potts:

Yes.

Alex Saenger:

That's interesting, because if you read what they say, they're at the point in their career where they've been doing it long enough they've got a surplus of leads. Now, there are a few different ways you can handle that, right? 1. You can just not service those people that you don't like. That would be dumb. 2. You could actually hand off some of those leads that are maybe on the lower bracket of your service market, either geographically or in terms of price point or something like that. You could hand those people off to a more junior agent in your office, that's just looking for business, and take a referral fee. 3. You might hand it over to one of your mentees. Somebody that you're mentoring already in the organization. 4. If you have a buyer's agent or somebody else that's licensed that's on your team, you could hand it off to them.

What if you don't have somebody like that on your team? Well, guess what, when you have a surplus of leads it's a great time to recruit somebody onto your team. Make sure you find somebody that's quality. Make sure it's somebody that wants to grow with your organization. Make sure that person has real talent. But, ultimately, bring that person onto your team, put together a handsome split for both of you, create a win-win, and that way you won't let those excess leads go dormant or be un-served.

Make sure that that team member you bring on fulfills the same level of service, the same culture, and the same expectation that you have for how you serve your clients, because your clients aren't necessarily just buying you. They're buying the systems and processes that you've put in place. That is really what defines the culture of your team.

So, if you've got excess leads, figure it out. Get somebody on your team. Get a great new team member.

Expanding Your Real Estate Team

Leo Robles, Corona, California

Leo Robles:

I would have hired an administrative person. Once I grew my business, I would have hired an administrative person faster. I got up to a hundred transactions and I was doing all of the work myself and I honestly would have done much better if I would have leveraged and started to build my real estate business as a business versus just continuing to plug away and sell real estate every single day.

Alex Saenger:

What Leo's really talking about can be summarized in The Millionaire Real Estate Agent book by Gary Keller. If you flip it open to page 202, you can actually see the progression of how you can build your business as a real estate agent. At the first level, you're working by yourself. At the second level, you're hiring an assistant. At the third level, you're splitting the assistant's responsibilities into two roles of marketing and transaction coordination. The point behind this is, when treating your business like a business, it makes a lot of sense to leverage talent that can actually help you expand your business more quickly.

And when you're ready for that next step, don't hesitate, because that assistant will actually help you double your business. Believe it or not, I did it and it worked, and I was amazed. And each person I added helped me double my business again.

How Hiring an Administrative Assistant Can Help Your Daily Work Flow

Arelis Perez, Upper Marlboro, Maryland

Arelis Perez:

I'm a very obsessive, over-the-top person with paperwork. If I spend most of my time doing administration, that means I'm not doing 80% of what I need to be doing, which is prospecting. Prospecting, prospecting, prospecting. Lead generation, lead generation, lead generation. So I've let go in that sense. I've got showing agents. I don't go to home inspections. I do show up for settlements.

Alex Saenger:

I can relate to what Arelis is talking about. When I was at my previous broker, they came to me and they told me, "Alex, you're really not good at turning in the paperwork, you're missing things." I was the worst person when it came to paperwork that was submitted. Ultimately they said, "You need an assistant." And I was like, "okay," and I wound up hiring an assistant and it changed my world.

Immediately, I turned from being the worst person with paperwork to being the best person with paperwork. Just by hiring the right person. Do you know what happened when I hired that person? I doubled my business that year. That's right, because I took away all those things I didn't like doing and I gave it to somebody who was better at it than I.

If you're struggling with something, maybe it's time for you to identify somebody else that can do that work better than you. Get that burden off your shoulders, so that you can double your business this year.

How to Curb Long-Term Costs by Hiring an Administrative Assistant

John Pace, Richmond, Virginia

John Pace:

It's scarier up front to hire an administrative assistant because you have a fixed cost now that you're paying for, versus a buyer's agent you just pay as a split. But, at the same time, you will pay a buyer's agent three or four fold of what you'll pay an administrative staff member, and that administrative person can really leverage you heavily to make a lot more sales. They can allow you to get focused on your 20%, which is selling homes. Of course, I screwed that up numerous times, and finally fixed that this past year.

Alex Saenger:

So, what John's talking about is pretty simple. The cost of an administrative person is more expensive up front, but the cost of a buyer's agent is more expensive long-term. Because a buyer's agent is going to cost you half of the commission, or 40% of the commission. If you're making a $10,000 commission on a $400,000 sale, you're just giving them about half of that money. That doesn't make a lot of sense, when you could have an administrative person to handle all of the administrative work. You're going out, and now you're actually making all that money. You might only be paying your administrative person $15-$20 an hour. It makes a lot more sense to hire an administrative person before you hire a buyer's agent.

Hire Talent

Liza and Tina Vernazza, San Carlos, California

Liza Vernazza:

We're hiring assistants sooner.

Tina Vernazza:

Yes.

Liza Vernazza:

We hire talent sooner.

Tina Vernazza:

Yes, talent, that's the real key thing, hiring good talent. She's about ready to move up to a buyer's agent.

Liza Vernazza:

So we're hiring talent.

Tina Vernazza:

We're hiring talent now.

Liza Vernazza:

Looking to hire talent, yes.

Tina Vernazza:

We're hiring her replacement right now. She can move on to selling and representing buyers and then that frees me up to deal 100% with sellers.

Liza Vernazza:

And I built all the systems that I'm going to be hiring somebody to continue working with.

Alex Saenger:

A couple of things that they talked about here are really important. One, if you're a new solo agent and you haven't hired your first assistant, hire that assistant as soon as you can financially afford it. Get that person in there as fast as you can, because that person is actually going to take off of your plate all those things that you hate doing. All of that administrative work and maybe some of the marketing work. Things that you maybe aren't as good at, or you can find somebody who is better at than you are, even if you like doing it. When you do that, trust me, you're going to double your business.

Now, in the process of hiring that person, it's very important to hire talent. Don't just fill that role with just somebody you picked up off the street. Make sure that you vet them extremely well. Go through the Career Visioning program at Keller Williams to help you figure out how to actually hire and build your team, and how to effectively identify and attract the people that are the right fit.

Next, make sure that you build a vision for your business. You build a world around your business that is so big that your team members will never want to leave. In the end, you're going to need to make sure that you incorporate, not just your vision of where you want to go, but their vision of where they want to go, and help your team grow to encompass their goals as well as your own goals. When you do that, guess what? They don't want to leave. They want to be a part of your team for as long as you'll have them, and as long as you're growing.

Hiring Personnel to Perform Tedious Tasks

Michael Acquisto, San Antonio, Texas

HIRING PERSONNEL TO PERFORM TEDIOUS TASKS

Michael Acquisto:

Use other people to do things that you don't feel like doing. Have somebody manage your contracts and do all of the dirty work on them. I mean, I spent way too much time in a computer typing in data. I hate typing in data on a computer. I really wish I'd had somebody that I could take the 100 business cards to, and have them put the email addresses in and do that work for me because that's something I hate doing.

Alex Saenger:

There's an old saying that goes, "If you don't have a maid, you are the maid." Another way to put that is, if you don't have an assistant, you are the assistant. So, ask yourself the question, what kind of work are you doing right now that you could delegate to somebody else that may be less expensive than you yourself? For example, is there some work that you could pay somebody minimum wage to do, for example, to take business cards and enter their information into a database or take contact information that you receive from somewhere and stick it into your database? That's probably not the best use of your time, but it is something that somebody else could do and can get you started much more quickly.

As another example, are you sending out mailings? Are you sending out 100 letters a month? If you're doing that, are you sitting there tri-folding those, sticking them in envelopes, addressing them, putting stamps on them, and taking them to the post office? What if you had a teenager at home that wanted a little bit of extra cash? Maybe they could handle your mailing, and you just have to bring the mailing home. Let your teenagers fold that letter up and stick it in an envelope or address the postcard, and stick the stamp on it. Let them take it to the post office. Instead of you doing this mundane task, you could spend your time connecting with people, shaking hands, rubbing elbows, and having those voice-to-voice or face-to-face conversations that could lead to that next piece of business. So, think about leverage and whom you know that can do some of those administrative tasks for you, so you can move forward with your business with more productive work.

Holding Your Team Members Accountable

Dan Burgess, Palo Alto, California

HOLDING YOUR TEAM MEMBERS ACCOUNTABLE

Dan Burgess:

By far and away, I'm kind of a nerd when it comes to these Keller Williams guys. They're all rock stars to me, but Ben Kinney is probably my favorite. I've gone to a couple of his sessions that he's taught over the last few years, and he's just an inspiration to everyone who's getting into business, whether you're in real estate or just an entrepreneur getting into anything.

One of the things he said was, control the people who are around you, and expect results from them. I really thought that stood out to me personally. Making sure that you really control your surroundings, and control who's around you, and hold them to the standards that you want to hold your business and yourself to, and then of course show them love when they do hit their mark.

Alex Saenger:

So, Ben Kinney is one of the all-time rock stars in the Keller Williams world. Why? Because he's figured the system out. He used to be a cable guy, and got to be this ginormous agent. And the way he did that, is by holding people accountable. Now, what does that mean, holding people accountable? That means, for example, if you have a standard of ten phone calls in a day, and the people on your team are only making eight phone calls, and there's no repercussion, or there's no reprimand for doing that, you effectively are telling people that eight is really our standard, because it's okay.

So, if you don't hold people to those standards, you're not going to get the results that you're expecting. Make sure that you yourself are accountable, and maybe you have some sort of consequence for yourself if you don't reach the goals that you have defined for yourself each day.

Why You Should Help Your Team Members Achieve Their Goals

Arnita Greene, Upper Marlboro, Maryland

Arnita Greene:

Getting that next step, maybe hiring an assistant, is sometimes hindered, because of course, you want all your money to yourself. That's what we always do, but that was my limited way of thinking, "I just want it just to be me all the time." No. I need to help somebody else and make their business better too, and they're learning from me.

Alex Saenger:

So if you have a team, and you're focused on expenses, like a lot of agents, you're going to have concerns. In fact, you are probably going to think something like this: "Wow, I have these expenses of these people and I'm struggling myself. How can I afford to pay them? How can I worry about their goals when I have to worry about my own goals? And now I have to worry about the team goals as well?"

But there's a funny thing that happens when you help your team members achieve their goals, they'll actually help you achieve your goals at an even higher level. You'll wind up making more money as an organization than you ever thought possible before. Why? Because you're actually helping, you're actually assisting, and you're actually giving those people incentive. You're inspiring them to want to be part of your team, to be part of your organization, and to see the organization succeed as a whole.

When you do that, you inspire people. You help them realize their dreams. And all of a sudden, they want to be part of what you're doing. They in turn, will help lift your business up and make you more successful. So achieve a higher level of accomplishment by helping your team members, and in turn, they will help you.

Leverage Yourself to Help Your Business

Carol Simenson, Bismarck, North Dakota

Carol Simenson:

Get your system. Try to leverage yourself as soon as possible. Back 23 years ago, it was all about the broker and agent, so there was no such thing as leverage and it didn't take me long to understand that I needed help. I needed somebody to assist me through the day.

Alex Saenger:

Elsewhere in this book, we talk about the triangle, the Millionaire Real Estate Agent fundamental triangle: leads, listings, and the third side of leverage, and that's what Carol is talking about. When you're building your team of individuals that are going to help you succeed in your business, you're going to probably go along the path that Gary Keller defined in his book, The Millionaire Real Estate Agent.

If you're interested in learning more about that, I definitely encourage you get a copy of the book.

The Importance of Working With a Team

Cheryl Coleman, Huntington Beach, California

Cheryl Coleman:

How to build a team and how important teamwork is should be understood. My last company wouldn't let me have a team. The broker said, "I make money off of individual agents. We don't have teams here." We do now. But without the teamwork, I couldn't be successful. I needed help. I needed a team, and Keller Williams is all about team, so that really helped me.

Alex Saenger:

When Cheryl talks about teams, it's really interesting. Some brokers, like she mentioned, are not interested in teams. What's funny about it is, if you look at The Millionaire Real Estate Agent book by Gary Keller, and you go to page 202, he talks specifically about the different types of teams that you can establish. By the way, at the first level it's just you by yourself. Everything else is really a team, even with just having one assistant, you now have a team.

So the fact that you understand how the different models are established for building a team, and what's the right hire at the right time, is super critical. If you haven't read the book, The Millionaire Real Estate Agent, I highly recommend it. It is one of the tools I used that allowed me to implement systems and models, even when it comes to building a team.

Why Finding a Partner Could be Your Key to Success

Jeanne Longueira, Garden City, New York

WHY FINDING A PARTNER COULD BE YOUR KEY TO SUCCESS

Jeanne Longueira:

It probably would have helped to meet my partner a little earlier. I think through a contribution between what he can do and what I can do, we actually took over an office, and we built it together. We have a great investor group too. All our hard work paid off. We would have created the team a little earlier, made our hires a little better, and sooner.

Alex Saenger:

So you can see that Jeanne really leveraged the collaborative potential of Keller Williams and built her team, first as a partnership, then an office, and then growing her team even more. So if you're looking to build that kind of an environment for your real estate practice and take your business to the next level, and then the next, you might want to think about talking to somebody at a local Keller Williams office. You might also want to think about reading Gary Keller's The Millionaire Real Estate Agent book. It talks all about how you can build your team the right way, the systematic way.

And when you are ready for that conversation, feel free to get in touch with me directly at IWantToJoin@RealAgentAdvice.com. Let's connect directly so we can have a conversation and see if your local KW office is the right fit for you. If it is, I would be thrilled to be your inspiration for joining. I would be honored to be your sponsor.

How Expanding Your Team Lays the Foundation for Retirement

Kelly Duncan, Longmeadow, Massachusetts

Kelly Duncan:

There are benefits to having a team. I have a team, but I think I would be long since retired if I had learned about teams earlier on. I think I would have grown. I would've started my own team and I would've been retired out of the business already.

Alex Saenger:

What I take away from what Kelly's talking about, is planning for your retirement as a real estate agent. A lot of agents don't really think about it. They're in the business. They're doing the business. They're doing transactions, but they're not necessarily thinking about where do I go from here? And at what point do I actually want to retire out of this business?

If you've been in the business for over 10 years, maybe 20 years, some people even 30 years, you might be getting to the point where you're thinking, "I really should start thinking about retiring."

So building a team is one of the things that allows you to start thinking about that. There are a lot of different models and a lot of different ways to do it. First things first, if you don't have an assistant, start there. Secondly, once you're doing more than let's say 24 or 48 transactions a year, in terms of listings, now you have enough business to start feeding a buyers' agent.

So building your business over time, allows you to build your team. Building your team, eventually allows you to think about starting your retirement.

Chapter Ten:

Coaches and Mentors

Introduction

If you are a real estate professional, there are two important kinds of people that you should get to know: coaches and mentors. They fill different roles, but both are invaluable to have. In this chapter, you'll learn about both.

You'll learn in this chapter about the role of a coach.

You'll learn that a coach is not someone who tells you exactly what to do, like a coach in a sport might call plays. You'll find out instead, that a coach's role really focuses on accountability. You'll discover that a coach will keep you accountable, remind you of your goals, keep you on track, motivate you, and steer you in the direction of success. You'll find out that a coach can teach you, help you through challenges, and bring out the best in you. You'll also understand that having a coach requires a commitment on your part.

This chapter also talks about mentors. A mentor has a different role than a coach and is also someone that you should get as soon as you can.

You'll find out that this is a person who can help you when you first start out in real estate. You'll discover that a mentor can teach you things, answer questions, and give you support. You'll understand that a mentor is a great person to have help you during your first transaction. You'll also discover that this is the kind of person that you want to learn from and lean on. From the advice you read, you'll realize that, if you are just starting out in real estate, you should get a mentor.

In real estate it is important to learn from someone. It is important to seek advice from successful seasoned agents. These people have done what you are endeavoring to do and have been successful at it. They can help you get where you want to go. Coaches and mentors are these people.

Hopefully, after you read this chapter, you'll seek out a coach, a mentor, or both. Your business will be better for it.

If you are a seasoned professional, you might consider becoming a coach or a mentor yourself. You will be able to help others and you yourself will grow.

How Coaching Can Help You

Susan Salazar, Franklin, Tennessee

Susan Salazar:

Get a coach. They say that again and again, but I didn't listen. It took me 13 years to get a coach. I finally did it this year and the business is starting to grow quickly. It's reminded me that I need to get back in contact with my database. The coach will help keep you on target, keep you on pace, remind you of your goals and why you set the goals that you did. They will push you to where you want to go. They'll just remind you and keep you accountable. Are you doing what you said you wanted to do?

Alex Saenger:

When you don't have accountability, when you don't have somebody watching over you, you can really get distracted, and you can really get off track. A coach is going to help you define what your goals are and what your business plan is, and a coach is going to hold you accountable to what you set as your goals for yourself and your business. Having a coach, having accountability, having your goals defined, and having your business plan established is going to allow you to shoot for the moon. And, even if you miss, you're still going to be among the stars. You may not quite hit your goal, but you're going to get a lot closer to your goal if you have accountability and you have coaching than if you didn't.

Knowing What Your Coach is Responsible For

Sujatha Bhaskara, Morganville, New Jersey

KNOWING WHAT YOUR COACH IS RESPONSIBLE FOR

Sujatha Bhaskara:

You know, one thing that I would do differently for sure is enroll myself in coaching, maybe the first year that I started. I met an agent who has only been in the business a year and he's already in Mastery Coaching.

Alex Saenger:

What is the job of a coach? The job of a coach is to bring the best out of you. So whether you're an athlete or whether you're a real estate agent, the job of a coach is not to tell you exactly what to do. A coach's job is to look inside you, see what potential you have, and bring that potential to the surface. If you're looking for a coach and you expect to be told exactly how to go from A to B to C to D, that's not the job of a coach. The job of a coach is actually to help you understand where you are, where you're going, and some of the things for which you have talent that are going to help you get there. Coaches are going to keep you on track, they're going to keep you accountable, and that's one of the reasons why Sujatha's talking about the idea that you might want to get a coach earlier rather than later. You might not feel like you have the money for it, but a good coach is going to wind up helping you build your business a lot faster than if you did it on your own. Coaches will pay for themselves several times over in a short amount of time.

If you're looking for a coach, and you're not sure where to start, get in touch with me. There are a lot of options out there. I can help you find the right fit. Just email me at coffee@RealAgentAdvice.com.

Coaching Breakthroughs

Mary Anne Walser, Atlanta, Georgia

COACHING BREAKTHROUGHS

Mary Anne Walser:

I'm in KW MAPS Coaching and it really does make a difference. You know what you're supposed to do and that's why I didn't hire a coach for a long time. I know what I'm supposed to do, the problem is doing it and you've got to be held accountable. It's not cheap, but there's something about paying that money each month, that made me think I was going to make that work. You know what I mean? If I'm going to pay that money, I'm going to make it work. With that commitment and with a good coach, I doubled my production my first year in KW MAPS Coaching. It was incredible.

Alex Saenger:

You know, when I first got my coach, I was really nervous about spending the money too. Once I got my coach though, I realized I needed that accountability. Most people think, "Oh, I just want to be free. I want to do whatever I want." But if you're going to be serious about this business, you need accountability to keep you on track and keep you focused on what's important. Someone who can help you avoid costly pitfalls and guide you on a path of success. That's going to make you the most money for your business or set you up to achieve the goals that you've set for yourself for the year.

View Feedback as a Gift so That You Can Excel

Catherine Delf, Latham, New York

Catherine Delf:

I got a coach and I have taken Train the Presenter twice now, I learned that feedback is just so powerful and it's a gift. When you view feedback as a gift, whenever anybody gives you any sort of advice, instead of getting down on yourself or getting really into your head, you can see it as a gift and you can just take it and move forward.

Alex Saenger:

What's an example of a piece of feedback that you looked at and said, "That was a gift."?

Catherine Delf:

To hold myself accountable to a schedule. To make sure that I'm not just flying around day to day, doing all the busy work of real estate, and really structure a business.

Alex Saenger:

So Catherine talked about a couple things there. Accountability is really at the core of everything she's talking about. Whether it be having a coach or getting feedback, they're all different forms of accountability. Without that feedback, without that coach, without the information to tell us what we're doing right and what we're doing wrong, it's really hard to improve. And ultimately, we all want to do better at our jobs and at life. Sometimes we're just scared to ask for that feedback or ask for that accountability because we don't want to be held to a different standard. We just want to do what we want to do. By getting that feedback, and by getting that accountability, we can improve, we can do better, and we can serve our customers better. We can serve our family better. And we can be more successful in our business.

You're Not Really a Professional Unless You Keep Score

Harrison Beacher, Washington, D.C.

Harrison Beacher:

Seek out a coach or mentor directly. I didn't really embrace that until five years into the business, and seeking out a coach or mentor to help me critique and focus on specific parts to improve was huge. The best thing my coach has taught me, is that you're not a professional if you don't keep score, and understanding what it means to keep score in terms of your appointments, your ratios, your numbers, and knowing your numbers.

Alex Saenger:

We're going to go back to The Millionaire Real Estate Agent book, and visit the "Economic Model"[14]. What Harrison's talking about is focus, and keeping score. If you don't keep score of what you're doing, there's no way to know how you're supposed to improve.

For example, if we look at the "Economic Model" on page 131, a number of specific items are listed. For sellers, they are: "seller listing appointments", the percent "conversion rate" of those appointments, the "seller listings taken" and the percent "conversion rate" for that, the "sellers sold", the "average sales price", the "seller sold volume", the percent commission, and then "gross revenue for sellers". These items are all in the figure for the model.[15]

We can look at each one of these different components, to see what your averages are in terms of conversion rates and, number of appointments. We can work backwards from there, and figure out exactly where you need to improve.

A coach is somebody that's going to help you refine that process, make sure that

---

[14, 15] The Millionaire Real Estate Agent by Gary Keller with Dave Jenks and Jay Papasan. Copyright © 2004 by McGraw-Hill Education

you have the tools you need to stay on track to meet your goals, and also help you identify the areas of your business that you need to improve upon.

It might be your rate of conversion from listings taken to listings sold. Maybe the issue there is your negotiation skills. Maybe you need to work better on that, or maybe it's something before you get to that point. Maybe you need to work on getting a better listing price.

Whatever it is, the numbers you record, the numbers that you capture, are going to help you focus on what you need to work on. A coach is somebody who's going to keep you accountable to those statistics and those numbers, to make sure that you're able to achieve your goals. A coach is more than you might think in terms of real estate. A coach is somebody that's going to make sure you're on track, and keep you heading toward your goals.

Why Using KW Productivity Coaching is a No Brainer

Kristin Rashid, Ann Arbor, Michigan

Kristin Rashid:

Be willing and open to learning at every opportunity you are given. For example, with Keller Williams, join the Productivity Coaching program. The Productivity Coaching program is something that our new agents all sign up for when they join Keller Williams and it's a program to get them into production within 90 days. It's giving them all of the tools to leverage their business and get them started.

Alex Saenger:

In the Productivity Coaching program, there's actually a manual. There is a class (well, a series of classes). There's a whole program designed to get agents up and running in the first 90 days to get them into production - meaning selling houses, getting leads, and making transactions happen. And not just get them up into production, but get them to the point where they're capping. If you don't know what capping is, you're probably not at KW, and you need to learn because you probably are paying your broker way more money than you should be.

Having a Coach

Richard Amato, Williston Park, New York

Richard Amato:

Having a coach helps me get through the days. It helps me hold my team leader accountable. It helps me hold my team accountable. It helps me. It gets me through a week, basically. It also, sometimes, is my therapist. When you have certain problems with other market centers, or other agents in the office, it helps you get through the day.

Alex Saenger:

Real estate is hard. It's a hard business. When people watch television, they often see all these shows about real estate that only show the glory moments. For instance, like when the negotiations happen, and when the deal closes, and how much money they made. They don't show the hard work that goes into actually doing real estate as a business though.

Having a coach is kind of like having a psychologist working on your behalf, but specifically focused on the business aspect of things. A coach's job is to help you get through the challenges of your week, and identify how you can move your business forward. A coach is someone that is on your side, is looking out for you, is in your corner, and wants you to succeed. It is invaluable to have somebody that you can talk to on a regular basis like that, where you aren't having just one conversation, but a series of conversations over time. The interaction is cumulative over time, and that's something important. Wow.

That can be a very powerful relationship that you can have with someone that's specifically related to your business, and to the strategies that you're trying to implement, to make your life a successful life, from a business perspective. This is not somebody like a spouse who is more concerned about what is happening at home. Coaches care about what you're trying to accomplish, and their job is to help you get there. They keep you accountable, bring you up when you need to be brought up, and make sure that you know that there's somebody always on your side that's going to encourage you to have a better day, and build a bigger business.

Why Getting a Coach Isn't Optional

Rich Ganim, Sarasota, Florida

WHY GETTING
A COACH ISN'T OPTIONAL

Rich Ganim:

What I would have done differently is, I would have hired a coach way sooner.

Alex Saenger:

It was short, wasn't it? Well, there's a reason for it. You need a coach. If you don't have a coach, go get one. If you are a coach, make sure you get all the rest of those agents that are under you up in the business. Bring them up.

Think about back when you were a kid or maybe you have children now and they were put on a soccer team and that soccer team played "pack ball". Do you remember that? They just kind of clustered around the ball? They didn't get anywhere because everybody was focused on and clustered around that ball.

It wasn't until a coach stepped in to say, "Hey, by the way, if player 5 comes over here, and you go over there, then when the ball is over here and everybody is starting to cluster around the ball, you can pass it to player 5. You can just pass the ball right around that cluster of players, and boom, you can get a shot at goal," that things changed dramatically.

It's a coach who sees things that you don't, who's been where you are now, and who can show you how to get to where you want to go. The job of a coach is to bring the best out of all the players, or out of the people who are being coached.

If you don't have a coach, make sure you get one so you can get the guidance you need to grow and become a better real estate agent. If you're somebody who has experience, and you don't have anyone you're coaching, you might want to think about doing so. There's somebody in your market center that could use your help.

Best of all, by helping others, you're going to grow from that experience just as much as they are. You might gain a friend, you might gain a coworker, or maybe help someone who then wants to join your team.

Grow a Thick Skin and Remember That Business is Business

Sally Masters, Naples, Florida

Sally Masters:

To get a coach, to get a mentor, to have somebody help you through the difficult times, and to grow a thick skin, and not take it personally are important. It's business. It's not personal. It's important to really step aside from the emotional side of real estate.

Alex Saenger:

I have a perfect example of this scenario, where an agent got really upset and emotional about a transaction. You see, I was a listing agent selling a house. The buyer's agent finished the walkthrough with his client. When they came out of the house, the buyer was visibly upset. The agent walked over to him and they spoke about the property. He came back over to me, and he started laying it on me about the fact that the toilet upstairs in the hallway was running. So I asked him to go get the disclosures. He got the disclosures and brought them back over to me. I flipped open the document, and I pointed right to the page where we disclosed the fact that the toilet leaked, prior to them even putting in an offer. When I gave that information to the agent, you could physically see his demeanor deflate. He walked over to his client, showed him the papers, and he deflated too.

It was really just a miscommunication and a misunderstanding. I told the agent, when I spoke to him, I said, "Look, this is not emotional for you and me. It's emotional for the buyer. It's emotional for the seller. As agents though, we're here to facilitate a transaction." So when it comes to your business, make sure that you treat it like a business, and your coach is the one that's going to help you do that.

How Mentors Can Help You as a New Real Estate Agent

Andrea Beem, Albany, Oregon

HOW MENTORS CAN HELP YOU AS A NEW REAL ESTATE AGENT

Andrea Beem:

A mentorship program. I didn't even realize what was available to me in terms of training, and in terms of helping my business get up and going. So it took me a full year to even think that I could be successful in this industry. It took a long time. The mentorship would have been a really big help to me.

Alex Saenger:

At Keller Williams, one of the things that we offer, actually the number one thing, is training. We have lots of training for new agents. We have a course called Ignite that goes through all the steps and processes you need to know about listings, buyers, contracts, and everything else to get yourself started in the real estate business. Training on databases, how to do an open house, and things like that.

Next, we have a Productivity Coach. The Productivity Coach is the person that will meet with you on a regular basis to help you get into production.

And then finally, we have mentors. People that, when you have a transaction and you're actually ready to do the transaction, you can talk to. What do I need to do in the paperwork? How do I negotiate with the other agent? How do I create a CMA (comparative market analysis)? How do I actually show clients what they should be paying for the house? All these different steps are what a mentor can help you with.

By understanding that you have those resources behind you when you first get started is such a critical element for a lot of new agents. Without having that support, they feel like they're scattered and on their own. If you're a new agent, make sure that you understand you have all those resources available to you.

Why You'll Need a Mentor to Help With Your First (Several) Transaction(s)

Jeff Tomlinson, Chicago, Illinois

Jeff Tomlinson:

If there's no Productivity Coach in your market center, find a mentor, and make that happen for yourself. You're going to need somebody to be on the phone with you when you write your first contract. It's not easy.

Alex Saenger:

As an experienced agent, one of the things that I offer to my market center is mentorships for newly licensed agents. It's really important to have somebody that's good, that you can trust, that is on your side. Someone who is also going to hold you accountable and steer you in the right direction to not only find the business but to actually conduct the business once you land it. Now, you're going to have to pay that mentor. In most cases, mentors receive a percentage of the commission so that they can get compensated for their time, because well, quite frankly, they're expensive people to hire.

The goal of the mentorship program is to get you up and running so that you can conduct business on your own. Through the process, you might discover that you and the mentor work really well together, and you might want to partner and become part of your mentor's team. If you're just getting started in real estate, and you're not sure where to begin, start by finding yourself a good mentor in your market center or in your office that can help you get up and running.

Find Your Mentors and Follow Everything They Do

Gloria Mendoza, Colorado Springs, Colorado

Gloria Mendoza:

An important thing, is probably hooking on to at least three seasoned real estate professions, and really declare that you're needy to them. Ask them permission for you to be able to call them at all times, at all hours of the day, because a lot of times, that's what's going to build your confidence. Through them, you have the answers, and that's going to help you in your business.

Alex Saenger:

As a new agent, one of the things that we always lack is experience. We have life experience, we have previous work experience, but we don't necessarily have experience in what we're doing right now as an agent.

Even if you do have two or three years of experience, you still don't know as much as some of the seasoned agents. Making sure that you attend special events like Mega Camp and Family Reunion at Keller Williams, are one way to connect with agents from across the nation.

But in your local market, in your market center or in your office, making sure that you are connected with agents that are high quality agents that have been there before, and have the experience to share with you and are willing to share with you, is really critical.

Now, one thing I will say, don't call them at all hours of the night. But you do want to have their permission to call them when you have something that comes up, or you might be able to stop by and visit them. For newer agents, you might even ask if you can shadow them for a day, maybe on a listing appointment or an open house or with a buyer consultation.

Shadowing Other Agents

Teresa Souvignier, Palo Alto, California

Teresa Souvignier:

At the beginning, I was very insecure about the contracts and the whole process. When you get your license, you learn how to pass the test, but you don't really learn how to do a transaction from start to finish. So, if I had to do it over again, I would shadow other agents. I'd even pay them to let me shadow them if they wanted me to, so that I could see exactly what they were doing, because it was for me to get my confidence to the point where I felt like I could tell people I knew what I was doing.

At the beginning, you're not doing very many transactions, so it takes time to really know what you're doing. And if you're not doing very many, you don't learn. So to be able to watch other people go through the whole process three or four or five times in a short period of time really would have helped me.

Alex Saenger:

One of the great things about Keller Williams, is that we have a lot of really great, talented individuals in every single market center. And those talented individuals, are, well, let's call them "seasoned", because they've been in the business for a while. The seasoned agents, typically are the ones that are going to be members of the Associate Leadership Council, or ALC. They're typically going to be the people that teach the Ignite classes. And they're also going to be people that can be mentors in step with a Productivity Coaching program.

Now the Productivity Coaching program is going to coach you on how to focus on lead generation and do things like that. It's going to be the thing that lifts you up and inspires you to go out there and get business. But a mentor is someone who's actually going to hold you by the hand and is going to help you through that actual transaction. When you have a piece of business, and you're thinking, "Oh my! I don't know what I'm doing," you're going to reach out to your mentor. "Hey. What should I be doing now? How can you help me figure this out? How can you help guide me through this process of actually working with this buyer or working with this seller and getting the transaction to settlement? Writing the contract, negotiating the contract. What should I say? I don't know what to say?" The mentor is the person that's going to be able to help you with that.

At Keller Williams, we have professional seasoned agents that are part of that program, and they're there to help. So if you're new to the business and you're thinking about where you might land, and you're not sure which brokerage you might want to go to, I would definitely encourage you to consider Keller Williams and feel free to name me as your sponsor. After all, you are reading this book this far, and I would say if you're thinking of joining, this book might have something to do with that. Right? And when you join, be sure to look me up in Kelle (the digital personal assistant from Keller Williams with artificial intelligence) and let's connect and send each other referrals! And maybe we will see each other at one of the national events!

Listen to Advice

Mary Anne Walser, Atlanta, Georgia

Mary Anne Walser:

Listen to people who have been successful in the business and believe what they say.

Alex Saenger:

Tell me more about that.

Mary Anne Walser:

I thought if you worked really, really hard, you'd be successful. As long as you put in the hours, you'd get there. To some extent that's true, but to another extent there are certain things you can do that can make you more successful in less time, and one of those was hiring an assistant. It took me way too long to hire an assistant.

Alex Saenger:

So what Mary Anne's talking about is listening to the advice of the people that came before you that have been successful. Real Agent Advice is all about that topic. We have interviewed over 100 people, from across the country, to bring you great advice that you can use in leveraging your own business, in your path, and in your business plan. The question is, are you going to do it? Are you going to take the time to read the interviews and implement the things that you learned?

Take the advice from all these great agents and make sure that you are leveraging the information and the lessons that they're able to teach you. After all, they made all the mistakes before you, to find success in the things that work, so you don't have to.

Chapter Eleven:

Choosing Keller Williams or KW

Introduction

Are you with Keller Williams? If you are, you made a smart choice. If you're not, you really need to consider it.

There are so many wonderful things about being with KW, that there are almost too many to list. In this chapter, you'll get just a glimpse of what KW has to offer.

You'll learn about the culture at KW, the training available, and the systems and models they have. You'll find out about your potential, the possibilities for business growth, and the possibilities for personal growth. You'll discover more about the different opportunities available and the potential for passive income opportunities. You'll learn that if other people can be successful, so can you. And that's just some of what KW has to offer.

It's difficult to describe all the benefits of being with KW. It's difficult to get the impact of the culture across in just a few words. It's tough trying to explain all that the training can provide.

In the interviews in this chapter you'll see a recurring theme. People love being at KW. People who started with KW are happy they did. People who didn't start at KW … wish they had.

If you are at KW, you know the benefits of being here. Hopefully this chapter will remind you of them, and maybe you can seek out new opportunities.

If you're not with KW, whether you're just starting out or you're with another firm, hopefully this chapter will open your eyes to just some of what KW has to offer. After reading it, you really should talk to someone who is at KW who can tell you more about what KW has to offer.

And when you do join, be sure to list me, Alex Saenger, as your sponsor. The first person to give you all this great advice packaged up in this great little book!

The Many Things KW Culture Can do For You

Gina Padro and Christine Whiteman, Garden City, New York

Gina Padro:

I have seen a major change in my business since joining KW a little over two years ago. I had been at other companies, large companies, independent companies, small companies, and startup companies. The training, the education and the technology that is available at Keller Williams has completely transformed both my business life and my personal life. And just the blessing of being with this company, is what has made me even more successful.

Christine Whiteman:

I can attest to this. I've known Gina for over fourteen years.

Gina Padro:

Yes.

Christine Whiteman:

And I've noticed a major change in her attitude, her outlook on life and everything, and I think it has a lot to do with the culture.

Gina Padro:

Yes. 100%.

Alex Saenger:

So a while back, I did a series about KW culture. And KW culture can be grouped into five different categories.

First, people come here to KW for the sharing. We all are an open book, we share

281

everything, and we even have open books at the market center so we can see what's going on with the money. But more importantly, as individuals, we share with one another.

Second, are our systems and models. We've mentioned before The Millionaire Real Estate Agent by Gary Keller. Guess what? All the systems and models are based on the things that he's researched and he's defined in that book.

Third is the training. The training is second to none. Keller Williams Realty, Inc. was named number one by Training magazine in 2017. They were number two the year before that. Think about that.

Fourth is E to P. What is E to P? Going from being entrepreneurial to being purposeful. Going from being this person who just really wants to focus on doing business, to being very purposeful and being very strategic about how you spend your time and how you grow your business.

And fifth is growth. We are a place where you come so that you can grow as an individual and as a team or in your business.

If you're thinking about a great place to do all of these things and you're looking for a culture that provides them, be sure to check out our culture series on Real Agent Advice and make sure that you listen to what Gina's talking about and follow her footsteps.

KW is the Bonus

Lela Rae Nemmers, Colorado Springs,
Colorado

Lela Rae Nemmers:

A bonus thing? Keller Williams is the bonus. There are no complaints. I have no complaints about Keller Williams. Keller Williams is definitely the bonus to me. My office is a bonus, the people there are a bonus, Family Reunions are a bonus, Mega Camps are a bonus, everything about Keller Williams is the bonus.

Alex Saenger:

Bonus. That's what she's talking about. Being at any brokerage, you're going to sell real estate. Being at any brokerage, you're going to have relationships with your clients. Being at any brokerage, you're going to have a commission, and a commission split. But the question is, what else are you getting from your broker? At Keller Williams, you get a culture that is unlike any other culture out there, at any other brokerage. That's not just at one office, it's across all offices across the nation. It's a culture of sharing, it's a culture of training, it's a culture of systems and models, it's a culture of growth, and it's a culture that takes you from being entrepreneurial to being purposeful.

That's why people come to Keller Williams, and all of those things are a bonus that come from being with a broker that's unlike any other out there.

It's Not What You Get … It's Who You Become

Angie Fucigna

Angie Fucigna:

Coming to Keller Williams has changed my life in a gazillion different ways. Mostly, it's my personal growth that I have gained and everyone that I've met on this journey. One of my favorite things that I heard all the time was, "It's not what you get … it's who you become."

Alex Saenger:

"It's not what you get … it's who you become." That's what she said. If you think about the path that you're on right now, you might be going it alone or you might be part of a team. But no matter what direction you're headed, or who you're going to be in real estate, you want to make sure that you surround yourself with extremely professional, extremely successful agents.

One of the things that I found in my time at Keller Williams, is that the more I get involved, and the more successful people I talk to, the more books I learn about. It's amazing that just listening to what they have to say about what they're reading can be a real dynamic change and shift in how you think. The person you become is partly about whom you meet, and with whom you surround yourself, and what you're reading.

I've read a number of books. Shift, The ONE Thing, The Millionaire Real Estate Investor, and The Millionaire Real Estate Agent are all examples. These are all books that Gary Keller, with others, wrote specifically around real estate. They're all books that I, before I came to KW, didn't really take the time to know, learn, or read.

When I went to Family Reunion this last time, there was a session where they talked about how to use The Millionaire Real Estate Investor book as a tool to recruit leads, to recruit agents, and to focus on building your business. When I did that seminar, I just signed up and said, "I'm going to do this." I put it on the calendar and started promoting it. I had no idea what I was going to teach. I went into the KW system, found the materials, had the book, and I basically went through it and said, "Okay, I can relate this to how I actually do my business. I can relate this to how I've invested in properties." I put together the presentation and boom, I wound up teaching other agents and I wound up picking up investors as clients. In fact, the very first one that I did where I had an investor show up, we wound up putting contracts on three properties in just 20 days.

Something like that is where you get to learn and you get to become a more educated or wiser person. It's changed who I am because it's allowed me to become what I want to be through the education, through the tools, and through the systems. Hopefully this book has been a little bit of inspiration for you. I hope you get to focus on yourself, where you want to go, and who you want to become.

There are so Many Opportunities

Ryan McHugh, Boca Raton, Florida

Ryan McHugh:

The opportunity here is incredible. There's way more of an opportunity path than at a normal office where you're either an agent or the manager. I found a team leader role. I have plenty of good friends that are Productivity Coaches, MCAs, DOFIs, KW MAPS Coaches, or BOLD coaches. There's so much more to this business here than anywhere else that we have to offer them.

So if just being an agent is not exactly right for you, there's so many other paths. And what I love about our company is that when we put the teams together, there are a lot of other models. There are places that are saying, "If you're not good at sales, you cannot succeed in this business." And you know, we have transaction coordinators, admins, assistants, and directors of operations that make $100,000 plus every year. And they would probably choose to never go sell a house, but they run massive, massive businesses, which is super cool.

Alex Saenger:

What Ryan said is great. At KW, there are many paths that you can take when you think about being a real estate agent or being involved in real estate. There's not just one path, of being an awesome agent. There are so many other things that you can do within the business of real estate.

You can focus just on buyers, just on sellers, just on the administrative, just on the marketing, on some of the logistics, or on some of the operations. You could even join an office as part of the back office staff doing accounting or recruiting. There are lots of paths that you can take when it comes to real estate, and not every position is made for every person. Myself, I'm better at the sales side. I'd much rather give some of the administrative stuff to somebody who's better at it than I.

So, if you're thinking about real estate, and you're thinking about getting a license, go ahead, because there's probably a place for you within the real estate business that fits your personality to a "T".

What is Profit Share?

Sarah Keller, San Diego, California

Sarah Keller:

It's really important to put the other agent's information on the accounting sheets, so that we know who you're working with. This is helpful for a couple of reasons. As far as profit share and building your downline, it benefits you to put the other agent's information in there because if you had a really good deal, you can let us know. We'll give them a call, our team leader will get involved with them and see if they'd be a good fit for Keller Williams. If they're a good fit for Keller Williams, you're going to get the credit for recommending a quality agent, for building our company, and you'll be rewarded with profit share forever if that agent joins our market center and is working.

Alex Saenger:

What is profit share?

Sarah Keller:

Profit share means, if your market center profits at the end of the month, about half of that money goes back to our agents who have built Keller Williams. If you bring someone into Keller Williams, you are their sponsor. With every closing we basically take a look at how much of the market center's profit that closing was responsible for, and the sponsor is paid out a portion of that amount. Basically, they're rewarded for every single closing for that agent's entire career at Keller Williams, for recommending them, for bringing them on, and for growing our market center.

Alex Saenger:

Everything that Sarah talked about is exactly right. It's one of the unique cultural aspects of Keller Williams that you get to decide with whom you want to be in business. That was the question that brought me to Keller Williams. When I was contacted by an agent, his name is Pat, and he called me while I was at another brokerage, and said, "You know Alex, I was thinking about my business, and I was thinking about who I'm surrounding myself with at the office. I thought, if I'm going to be in business with somebody, who would I want to be in business with? Your name is one of the people that came to mind." And I thought, "You know what? I feel the same way about him. If I was going to share a business, is this somebody that I'd actually want to be in business with?" The answer was yes.

We talked a little bit more, I learned about the profit share and other things about Keller Williams, and once I realized that, I decided, "You know what? I do want to come here." Then, when I came I was blown away with everything else that it meant for me, because what he said to me was, "Alex, does it matter how much money you're giving your broker if I can show you how to double your business? And by the way, we also have a cap. Meaning there's a ceiling on how much money you'll give the broker in a given year." I said, "What? First, there's a cap? Second, you're going to help me double my business? Third, I'm actually going to get profit share in terms of just working with people I like? Working with them and encouraging them to come with me?"

When I started adding up all the financials about why I should come to Keller Williams, I suddenly went, "Why would I go anywhere else?" I'm so glad I came, and quite frankly, the only reason I'm upset is that I didn't come sooner.

I've got Something I can Share With You

Cheryl Coleman, Huntington Beach, California

Cheryl Coleman:

I actually sold all my 18 homes with Keller Williams. But back in the day there was no training. It was pretty much, let me get my license and go figure out how to do it. And I remember crying. I thought I'd gotten my first listing and I didn't, and it was so hard. So I ended up teaching and helped train, but then Keller Williams came and then there was just so much to share. You know? I just learned so much.

Alex Saenger:

So what's interesting about Cheryl's story is that it's very similar to mine. Before I came to KW, I was at a small boutique brokerage. And even before that, I was actually at a local, regional, powerhouse. What I realized there, was that there wasn't actually a culture of sharing and training. And it was something that I was personally looking for. It's actually how I discovered Brian Buffini's organization, Buffini and Company. I signed up and learned how his systems and models were able to teach you how to work by referral.

Then, when I went to the boutique brokerage, I realized, you know what, I actually knew a lot more than a lot of the people around me, and I was one of those people that was willing to share. I wound up meeting with a lot of folks, a lot of agents, and working and training them one on one.

I remember Ron Walton was one of the folks that I talked to. I actually just talked to him recently. He said, "You know what, Alex? One of the things I always remember about you, is when I joined the brokerage, you were the only one that actually came over to me and said, "You know what? Here, I've got something that I can share with you. Why don't you just implement this?" And it really stuck with him.

When I discovered KW, it was amazing. Now, all of a sudden, I was surrounded by people who had the same philosophy I had. I realized that we're not in competition with one another, because the fact of the matter is, you know different

289

people than I know. And the few people that we might actually know together, well guess what, one of us is going to have a better relationship with them than the other.

So, we're not really in competition. What we are is kind of like a family that wants to learn, and share, and teach one another, and bring new people into our lives that we can learn from. So, if you're thinking about where you might want to end up as far as a brokerage, and even if you're somewhere else right now, and you really want an environment where you can share and you can learn and you can train other people, you might want to consider KW.

If They Can Do It, We Can Do It Too!

Maria Hurtado, Yuma, Arizona

Maria Hurtado:

Come with Keller Williams. Come on board. They can do it. If they did it, we can do it too.

Alex Saenger:

What Maria had to say was very short but it was actually very powerful, and that is, "They did it, we can do it too." Now what does that mean? The reason Keller Williams has become the biggest real estate brokerage in the entire world, is because Gary Keller took the time to meet with 100 top agents from across the country. He listened to them, he took what they had to say, and he culminated those ideas into systems and models that are proven. The things that everybody can look at and point to and say, "If I do what those people did, I can be a huge success."

The same thing is true of the interviews in this book and at Real Agent Advice. Granted, they are not as profound and well researched as Gary's book, but what I did with those interviews, is I interviewed over 100 agents from across the nation, from various levels of skill and various levels of experience. What you'll find is that there are some common themes, regardless about whom we are talking. That's why you see some of the people showing up multiple times in different categories. Guess what? There's a pattern. If they can do it, so can we. So follow the models, follow the systems, and read the insights. If you haven't gotten Gary's book, The Millionaire Real Estate Agent, get it because it's a great platform to build your business from.

Follow the Systems and Models

Sarah Keller, San Diego, California

Sarah Keller:

You can get as much as you want out of Keller Williams. Not only do we offer all the tools and support that you guys need or ask from us, we really model what we're telling you guys to do. So Keller Williams International models how each market center is supposed to be run and each market center is kind of run like a mega agent would run their team.

So if you follow the Keller Williams systems and models, you will be successful. You will be able to grow a big team and earn positive income through your team and through profit share.

Alex Saenger:

So what's interesting about what Sarah talked about, is that Keller Williams has a model specifically designed to show how to best run your real estate business. If you think about that, why is that the case? Well Gary Keller took the time to interview 100 of the top agents from across the nation, from across all brokerages. He came up with what are the commonalities between all those agents. He then took that and created models from which he built his business. Those models then trickled down to each individual market center, or office, and those offices are run the same way.

Each agent team in an office runs its business the same way. And individual agents should run their businesses the same way. That last piece is usually where things fall apart. Because agents aren't following the models. But once they start to follow the models, then they wind up building a team. And once they build a team, then they're given the opportunity to open up different market centers and different offices. And they can actually become operating principals or generate revenue from those offices. Then they can expand their teams, with expansion teams, all using the same model that starts from the very top all the way down to that individual agent.

If you're interested in learning more about these models, get a copy of The Millionaire Real Estate Agent. You can go to www.alexsaenger.com/books/ which is a great place for you to get a copy of the book and if you do go to that, guess what? I'll make $1 every time you buy a book. So if you want a copy of The Millionaire Real Estate Agent book, just go to www.alexsaenger.com/books/. Or if you want to order more copies of this book, do the same.

Grow Faster With KW's All Inclusive Training

Dean Ueda, Honolulu, Hawaii

Dean Ueda:

I hate to sound like I'm trying to sell Keller Williams, but I wish someone had told me about Keller Williams, because I actually found them last. I found Keller Williams last, after interviewing all the other brokerages in my market. Keller Williams was the last one I went to, and I'm very happy I went with them. The amount of training ... it was actually the training that they offered that sold me. So make sure you look for a company that has the training to offer you.

Alex Saenger:

So just like Dean, I discovered KW last. Do you know why it's last? Because you stop once you get there. Ultimately, I came to Keller Williams, and the only reason I was upset when I came? That's right, you know the answer ... I was upset that I hadn't come sooner. I started off my career with a big regional broker, then I went to a boutique broker. Ultimately in both places I realized that what I was missing was training.

I actually went out and sought out training while I was there on my own, and I had to go outside of the company to get the training that I needed to fulfill my goals for my business. When I came to KW, I realized that all the training that I needed and wanted was actually within the company. It allowed me to lean into the system, learn the system, and even travel across the country and go to different events that had the type of training that I was looking for.

Chapter Twelve: **Bonus Interviews**

Introduction

In putting together the chapters for Real Agent Advice, there were several interviews that were important but didn't fit within the main structure of the book. These miscellaneous interviews made us think, "BONUS"!

In this bonus chapter, you'll learn about a variety of different topics. You'll learn about:

- Being an agent in Costa Rica
- Disbursements
- Investing
- Persistence
- Achieving goals
- Expansion

Enjoy these bonus interviews.

Become a Trusted Local Resource

Gina Briguglio, Playa Flamingo, Costa Rica

Gina Briguglio:

One of the most unique things that I do is, not only do I sell property in Costa Rica, but I also help and that's part of the reason I'm here today. They come to Costa Rica and they purchase. Then they call me when they get back and say, "Oh my! Now I have to sell my house!" So helping them on both ends, in two different countries, is one of the big things that I do. I'm selling an entire lifestyle. I'm not selling a home. I'm selling a whole new life to people, so not only do I sell them, but I help them transition in with things like immigration, taxes, attorneys, where to go, or where to buy their car. So I assist people in every way out there.

Alex Saenger:

So the lifestyle in Costa Rica might be a little bit different from where you live, but the one thing that's consistent, whether you're in Costa Rica or in the U.S., is that you can be the local expert that your clients can call on to find out whatever they're looking for. Whether, in her case, they're things like immigration or where to find a car, or in your territory, where does a person go to find the closest coffee shop or maybe a great place to have a car fixed, whatever it is, you want to be that local resource. You want to be that connector between people and the information, people, and services they're looking for. If you're not doing that now, you might want to think about it. If you are doing it now, you might want to consider upping your game and putting together a referral directory.

Being the person that everyone can go to when they move to an area is one of the most important and valuable things we can do, and it doesn't cost us anything. It also provides the opportunity to send referrals to service providers who then, in turn, will want to do the same.

How KW Helps You Get Your Money Faster

Sarah Keller, San Diego, California

Sarah Keller:

So, we do DA's, which are Disbursement Authorizations for commissions. Basically, at the opening of escrow, Keller Williams has this thing they call the Greensheet. It has all the financial information that we need for our market center (office) to know that a deal is happening. Things like total commission amounts, sales prices, basically all the information I'm going to need. I create the DA. That gets sent to escrow (the escrow and title company) so that escrow knows at closing the total commission amount that is going to be disbursed to all the parties involved. This goes to our market center for the commission split to the agent and the broker. If it's a team deal, we make sure both agents involved get their split.

So at close of escrow, the escrow and title company will cut us five or six checks, all to the exact amounts. This has been verified throughout to be correct. Everyone is getting paid the right amount. So the day a transaction or sale closes, we can just distribute checks right away at the settlement table.

Alex Saenger:

And what does that mean for the agent?

Sarah Keller:

For the agent, it means they get paid right away. They get paid the correct amount. Their cap is being calculated correctly, and they can make sure they're getting paid on time for the amount that they're supposed to.

Alex Saenger:

And when do they receive that check?

Sarah Keller:

They'll receive it as soon as escrow gives it to us. So usually it's carried over, so pretty much the day of close of escrow. If it's before noon, they'll get the check that day.

Alex Saenger:

So the interesting thing about Keller Williams, and I never knew that this was even possible, is that prior to going to settlement, and in fact, right until your property goes under contract or goes into escrow (whichever you use in you market area), you can create what's called a Greensheet. And that Greensheet gets submitted to the market center administrator. That person actually will take those numbers and make sure that all commissions are defined correctly. Most importantly, they're going to create something called a disbursement authorization or a DA. Now that DA is your best friend when it comes to settlement. Why? Because your DA is the thing that allows the settlement company, or the title company, to actually write a check to you in your name at settlement.

This means you don't have to wait for that check to come in and be processed through your office. You can actually get that check right at settlement, made in your name. You can take it to the bank the day of settlement. Or you can use an app like I do and just deposit it to your bank account literally right after settlement in your car. It's one of the unique features about Keller Williams, and it allows you to speed up that process so that you get your money faster.

Real Estate: The Investor in You

Wendy Papasan, Austin, Texas and Kymber
Menkiti, Washington, D.C.

Wendy Papasan:

We have a unique opportunity as real estate agents. We have kind of an inside
track to buy great investment properties. We also have an obligation as fiduciaries
of our clients to learn about real estate investing and to teach it to our clients. If
we can do that, not only can we build our own wealth, but we can help generations
of people become wealthier.

Kymber Menkiti:

Absolutely. I think that the key to starting ... a lot of people ask us, "How did you
move when you saw the final picture?" But the reality is that it started by really
focusing on how to spend less than you make.

Wendy Papasan:

Yes.

Kymber Menkiti:

And invest the rest wisely.

Wendy Papasan:

Yes, exactly.

Kymber Menkiti:

So, we lived in a very modest first home and we rented it out. We bought another
home and we didn't drive tons of cars. We really controlled our lifestyle so that

we could invest in the things that created a bigger return for us.

Wendy Papasan:

Yes, most people will never sacrifice today to get something in the future. Actually, there's a term for it. It's called, "hyperbolic discounting". If you ask someone this question, "If I had $100, and I could either give it to you today or I can give you $200 in a year, which would you choose?" There's the idea that a large percentage of people would take the $100 today.

Kymber Menkiti:

Give me the money.

Wendy Papasan:

Yes, but in reality, if it's $200, why wouldn't you wait a year? You make twice as much money?

Alex Saenger:

So this particular interview was conducted at the Regional Mastermind here in Washington, D.C. Wendy flew in from Texas to specifically talk about the path of money, which can be found in The Millionaire Real Estate Investor book. As it so happens, Wendy's husband is Jay Papasan, who actually co-wrote the book (along with Dave Jenks) with Gary Keller. What's amazing about her story, is that she and her husband really came from basically almost nothing, and they have amassed millions of dollars in personal wealth over just a short period of time. Probably about five to eight years.

Bo Menkiti, Kymber's husband, is the founder of Keller Williams Capital Properties, the brokerage that I actually work with. They now have seven offices here in the Washington, D.C. metro area. Again, building a path of wealth.

When you look at some of the things they're talking about, that are defined in The Millionaire Real Estate Investor book, and you focus on cash flow, it's really interesting to look at how consumers spend their money when they get it and how investors spend their money when they get it.

Basically investors are going to invest first and then worry about their expenses later. Consumers are going to consume money first and whatever's left over, that's what they're going to wind up investing.

The example that these women gave, the, "would you take $100 today or would you wait a year to get the $200?" Well, the answer should be that you'll wait a year to get the $200, because you're going to get twice as much money. But people are focused on consuming that money right away and they're not thinking about the long term impact of what that money can actually do for them or what their decision today means for them in the long term.

It's a really interesting perspective when it comes to real estate. And part of what they're talking about, is as real estate agents we have a fiduciary duty to our clients to help them understand this. Sometimes, the best decision is not to sell the house. Especially, if you can afford the next one without selling it. Sometimes the best decision is actually to hold onto that house, because it's a great investment long term.

In fact, I teach a Millionaire Real Estate Investor workshop or seminar every month and during that seminar I talk about the fact that in just seven years you can probably pay for your kid's college education with just a $50,000 down payment, buying a $250,000 house. I know, because I've actually done it. I've done the investment. I held a property. Now I've got money that's sitting around that's actually going to pay for my daughter's college education. Now I just have to figure out how to pay for the other two ;-)

A Professional Will Work Until They Can't Get It Wrong

Dianna Kokoszka, Austin, Texas

Dianna Kokoszka:

An amateur will work until they get it right. A professional will work until they can't get it wrong. Which one are you going to be?

You got into real estate for one of three reasons. 1) You got in for freedom, 2) for flexibility or 3) for the financial reasons. Now, let me tell you, ladies and gentlemen, you'll never make your financial goals if you take freedom and flexibility first. You only get the freedom and flexibility because you literally did the financial first

Alex Saenger:

Dianna talks about the three F's: freedom, flexibility, and financial. We can also translate those into three P's of real estate. First you have to prioritize, followed by becoming professional, and that's going to lead you to becoming profitable. If you do those things, you're going to have that freedom you're looking for in the end. That's why you got into the business after all. Follow Dianna's advice. You'll become profitable and then you'll have the freedom and the three F's that you're looking for.

Where do You Want to be in Five Years?

Chris Upham, Northern Virginia

Chris Upham:

I heard Gary Keller say, "You're only five years away from being whoever you want to be and accomplishing whatever you want to do." It was interesting, Leo Pareja has accomplished tremendous amounts of things, and each of those things have come in about five year cycles.

He built a real estate team to the seventh level and sold that and turned it over to someone else, in five years. He built a hard money capital private equity fund and turned that over seventh level to someone else running it, in five years. He's now in the technology business, and by the way doing some amazing things that he's rolling out to all agents through the MLS, and he's two years into that and is about three years away from completing that project.

What I take away from that, is I've spent fourteen years doing much of the same things over and over again, whereas Leo Pareja really recognized what were his limitations, what were his weaknesses, and found the right people to turn those over to. I think that one of my biggest challenges is I'm good enough at a lot of things that I keep my hands in the middle of and don't turn them over. It's not a new "aha." It's something I've known for a long time. Something I'm working through in my own life and business growth is getting the right people, the right talent around me, so that they can take those things further than I'm able to do on my own.

Alex Saenger:

So, you're only five years away from accomplishing any real goal that you want to accomplish. It's really just a matter of starting with what the goal is in mind and kind of working backwards. What do I need to do to accomplish that goal? What do I need to do to accomplish that four years from now, three years from now, two years from now, and then what can I do today to get to that goal? What am I missing? Who are the people I need to be introduced to? What are the skills that I need to learn? What's the education I need to have? Understanding where you want to go, building that goal, building that dream, and then working backwards to figure out what do you need to do today is a great place to start with your business.

Expansion

James Nellis II, Fairfax, Virginia

James Nellis II:

Expansion. I love expansion. We're a part of expansion. I hired an expansion director this last year.

But in general, expansion is just the opportunity really for us to run many brokerages throughout the country with people that we see of value. We love to grow them from inside, for them to reach such a high level, like there's almost no top that they can't pass. So we allow them to go to another market, into another market center, and really expand their own business. Expansion is a business within a business, and so the truly talented people never have to leave the team

Alex Saenger:

What is expansion? So, we've talked about The Millionaire Real Estate Agent book, and one of my favorite pages is page 202. It shows the organizational model. By the time you get to the bottom of this model, at the seventh level, you realize, "Wow, I built this great business, I've really honed in on the people that I need and everything else, but there's something more. There's something bigger." So the seventh level is getting to that. The highest level in the model, the eighth level, which is going to be in the next book that Gary puts out, the next version, is actually expansion.

What is expansion? It's where you take the business model that you've created, that's successful in your little local market and you start repeating it in other areas and other territories. Most people actually start from their central hub, wherever they live and they start branching out from there. So I'm in Rockville, Maryland in the Washington, D.C. metro market. I might decide to do an expansion into eastern Maryland at the beach. I might decide to do an expansion in the Baltimore area or near Deep Creek Lake. I'm just going to kind of swell out from where I am once I've built the systems and tools and models that work for me in my business to genuinely and specifically generate repetitive leads and have a great lead generation system. Now I can repeat that process throughout my marketplace. Also, if I find someone who's talented, someone who's really good at real estate, but maybe they haven't created those systems and the models, and they want to have a business within the business, it might mean an expansion team within our own team. They can maybe open up something at Ocean City, Maryland, on the beach.

So, once you've defined your models, you can then have the opportunity to attract talent. Put those two together, and that's when you can actually have an expansion team and expand your business. It's something that most brokers don't talk about. In fact, I don't know any other broker that talks about expansion like Keller Williams does.

Conclusion

It's not often in life that you get an opportunity to sit down in a room and learn from over one hundred people who are doing what you're doing and have been where you've been. It's not often that you get the perspective of those just starting out and those who have reached success. It's not often that you get really good advice, from really good people. But that's what Real Agent Advice is all about.

You've just had an opportunity to sit in a room and learn from over one hundred professionals. You've learned about everything from the basics of business to generating leads to having the right mindset. You've learned from people just like you and people who are where you want to be.

As you think about all that you have learned, remember, Real Agent Advice is a beginning. The insights you have been provided should inspire you to change the way you do business. They should inspire you to go to the next level. A door has been opened for you – it is time to walk through.

Keep Real Agent Advice on your desk. Refer to it often. If you are wondering about something or you feel like you just need something to kick start your day, turn to it. Each time you read an interview you'll gain a new perspective and new inspiration, the first time, the second time, each time. Because you are now in a different place in your business. Each time you look at the material you are using a different lens and you have a different perspective.

Don't keep Real Agent Advice to yourself though. Share it with others. Share it with those in your office. New agents and seasoned professionals alike can benefit from it. It is also a great tool for coaches and mentors to share with those they are working with. Additionally it's a great book for other business professionals because the insights apply to more than just real estate. It's a way for you to share the insights of dozens of professionals with one small act.

In addition to the professionals interviewed in this book, you also have gotten to know Alex Saenger. Because of Alex's hard work and dedication to helping others, Real Agent Advice has been brought to you.

The first sentence of Alex's business philosophy is "Our business is focused on you". As you've seen from all that Alex has put into this book, the sharing of his insights, and how he's been able to connect with people all over the country, that "you", isn't limited to just his clients. Alex is focused on you, the real estate professional, as well.

Alex is all about helping others. If you know someone moving into or out of the Washington, D.C. metro area, give Alex a call at 301-200-1232. He is never too busy for a referral or an introduction, and always looking to help where he can.

If you'd like to reach out to Alex, to let him know what you thought of the book, share an insight you have, or just have coffee, you can email him at coffee@realagentadvice.com. Alex would love to hear from you.

Finally, thank you for reading Real Agent Advice. Because of that simple act alone, you have made this project a worthwhile success.

Index of Interviewees

Index

Other Resources

In Real Agent Advice you read about a number of books. Some of them include:

The Millionaire Real Estate Agent by Gary Keller with Dave Jenks and Jay Papasan

The Millionaire Real Estate Investor by Gary Keller with Dave Jenks and Jay Papasan

The One Thing: The Surprisingly Simple Truth Behind Extraordinary Results by Gary Keller with Jay Papasan

Shift: How Top Real Estate Agents Tackle Tough Times by Gary Keller with Dave Jenks and Jay Papasan

These books can serve as great resources for anyone interested in learning more about real estate. You can purchase these books, other books, and additional copies of Real Agent Advice, by visiting www.alexsaenger.com/books/ and clicking on the book images.

Made in the USA
Columbia, SC
08 February 2019